∾

Breastfeeding and
Catholic Motherhood

Sheila Kippley

Breastfeeding and Catholic Motherhood

God's Plan for You and Your Baby

SOPHIA INSTITUTE PRESS®
Manchester, New Hampshire

Sophia Institute Press®
Box 5284, Manchester, NH 03108
1-800-888-9344
www.sophiainstitute.com

Library of Congress Cataloging-in-Publication Data

Kippley, Sheila.
    Breastfeeding and Catholic motherhood : God's plan for you and your baby / Sheila Kippley.
        p. cm.
    Includes bibliographical references.
    ISBN 1-933184-04-3 (pbk. : alk. paper)
    1. Breast feeding. 2. Breast feeding — Religious aspects — Catholic Church. I. Title.

RJ216.K498 2005
649'.33 — dc22   2005002217

05 06 07 08 09 10 9 8 7 6 5 4 3 2 1

Dedicated to Pope John Paul II
for his efforts to promote breastfeeding
and the welfare of the family

∞

Contents

∞
Appendix

∞

Foreword

This book is the fruit of John and Sheila Kippley's many years together as husband and wife, and of their ceaseless efforts as active promoters of natural methods of birth regulation and the time-proven benefits of breastfeeding.

It is a well-known scientific fact that breastfeeding, and especially ecological breastfeeding, has brought substantiated positive results in babies' health in defending against certain childhood illnesses and in helping infants grow and develop better. In addition, it brings long-term psychological benefits to the growing child. As for the mother, prolonged breastfeeding is also associated with positive effects on her general health.

In the overall picture, it is especially the nurturing of the close mother-infant bond that is so fundamental for the child's serene general growth and development. This aspect is of utmost importance today. At a time when the family is under attack, and the act of procreation is being constantly manipulated, this book affirms the continuity of the mother-child relationship from the womb, to the breast, and in the family. In this regard, the Holy Father himself did not hesitate to raise his voice in defense of this most honorable task entrusted to mothers:

> In the family, which a woman establishes with her husband,
> she enjoys the unique role and privilege of motherhood. In

a special way, it belongs to her to nurture the new life of the child from the moment of conception. The mother in particular enwraps the newborn child in love and security, and creates the environment for its growth and development. Society should not allow woman's maternal role to be demeaned or count it as of little value in comparison with other possibilities. Greater consideration should be given to the social role of mothers, and support should be given to programs that aim at decreasing maternal mortality, providing prenatal and perinatal care, meeting the nutritional needs of pregnant women and nursing mothers, and helping mothers themselves to provide preventive health care for their infants. In this regard attention should be given to the positive benefits of breastfeeding for nourishment and disease prevention in infants as well as for maternal bonding and birth spacing.[1]

Reconnecting with John Paul II's "theology of the body," Sheila Kippley also proposes a few thoughts and meditations for breastfeeding mothers who wish to find spiritual nourishment and encouragement from the Church in their most important task. This maternal attitude helps in expressing tenderness and in creating a more normal relationship that also contributes to the integral development of children in the dialogue of love that began even before birth.[2]

+Alfonso Cardinal López Trujillo
President, Pontifical Council for the Family
Vatican City, December 2004

∞

Introduction

The purpose of this book is to provide Catholics with scientific and spiritual support for breastfeeding. Of course, the many benefits of breastfeeding apply to all mothers, whether believers or atheists. But this book is addressed especially to Catholics. I will be quoting popes, bishops, priests, and others representing the Catholic Church to convey the Church's long-standing support for breastfeeding. And I hope to show how breastfeeding is an integral part of the vocation of Christian motherhood.

Today we have more clinical research than ever to support breastfeeding, much more than I had when I began my family in the Sixties. The spiritual approach to breastfeeding is less well known, but it is also important, and dedicated Catholics especially may find it interesting and compelling.

I am well aware that bottle-feeding is still the norm in America. Many people might ask, "If breastfeeding is so good, then why didn't my mother breastfeed me?" My mother breastfed me for only a few days. I don't blame her for not having breastfed me longer, nor should you blame your mother for not having breastfed you. Remember that the cultural influences in our society against breastfeeding, especially extended breastfeeding, have been very strong. Secondly, in our bottle-feeding society, the correct information and support for breastfeeding was often lacking and still is.[3]

This is not a book on how to breastfeed. Fortunately, there are many books, organizations, and professionals to help women succeed at breastfeeding. Nor is this a book on parenting. The principles of breastfeeding are compatible with many parenting styles, and good parenting books, including specifically Catholic parenting books, are easily available. Also, I have already covered some parenting advice and the topic of natural mothering in my book *Breastfeeding and Natural Child Spacing*.[4]

No, the main purpose of this book is to show the spiritual dimensions of breastfeeding; how breastfeeding is a natural, healthy part of being a Christian woman, mother, and wife.

Today many teachers of Church doctrine regarding sexuality make use of the "theology of the body" and the idea of the marriage covenant. These concepts can be applied to breastfeeding as well. The theology of the body was developed by Pope John Paul II to affirm and explain the self-giving nature of marriage and marital sexuality. Breastfeeding is an act in which the mother's body becomes a gift of self to her baby. In addition, the mother makes a "covenant" with, or unspoken commitment to, her baby through the devoted task of breastfeeding him over a period of time. In the traditional mother-baby breastfeeding relationship, mother and baby are inseparable.

Another theme that runs throughout this book is the importance of the mother's remaining with her child during the early years of life. This mother-baby togetherness is the common practice in societies where traditional breastfeeding is practiced. This special togetherness occurs naturally with breastfeeding, as God meant it.

There are two points concerning the text. First, you may find some additional information in the endnotes to be of interest. Commentary related to the text was added to the endnotes in each section or chapter. Second, masculine pronouns are used to differentiate the baby from the mother. With the topic of breast-feeding, mother and baby are mentioned often; using *he*, *him*, or *his* for the baby and *she* or *her* for the mother helps to avoid confusion.

If the information in this book encourages more mothers to nurse their babies, or to nurse for a longer period, the effort to write and publish it will have been worthwhile.

∽

Breastfeeding and
Catholic Motherhood

Chapter One

∽

The Health Standard
for Mother and Baby

God the Creator has a plan for all men, women, and children, and this plan applies to every area of our lives. When we learn and follow that plan, we are happier.

For example, if we discover and follow the rules for good nutrition, we will enjoy better health than if we don't. If we follow God's moral law, we will have happier relationships and peace in our hearts. God's plan extends to the conception and nurturing of babies as well. Through God's design, the mother's pregnant body nourishes and protects her baby during the first nine months of life. After childbirth the mother's body continues to nourish and protect her baby for many more months through breastfeeding. The repeated act of breastfeeding provides food for the baby — human milk, which is more nutritious than any other milk or food that a newborn might consume. Breast milk is not only the best nourishment for the baby, but the act of breastfeeding also provides the best nurturing environment for him. When a mother nourishes her baby at her breasts, she provides a safe and protective environment and the gift of her own personal presence, so important during the early years.

Breastfeeding is a natural process; the mother uses her own God-given natural equipment: her breasts to nourish and comfort her baby; her arms, her back, and her front or chest to carry him; and

3

her lap and her arms to hold him. Remaining physically close to her baby, the mother follows his cues with regard to his hunger, his tiredness, his alertness, his playfulness, and his need to be comforted. She also avoids the regular use of bottles and pacifiers.

Mothers may choose variations from this type of mothering, of course. Whatever specific parenting choices you make, the goal for successful breastfeeding is to nurse frequently enough to maintain an adequate milk supply for the baby. Parents must realize that supply follows demand and that when they reduce the opportunities for suckling, the milk supply may be reduced.

∞

Breastfeeding follows the biological laws

The natural processes of the body are often referred to as "biological laws." The Church has spoken frequently of the biological laws and encourages us to respect and follow them.

In 1960, Pope John Paul II (then Bishop Karol Wojtyla) wrote in his book *Love and Responsibility* that man's actions "must be in harmony with the law of nature."[5] In this book, the Pope wrote:

In the world of human beings the dictates of the natural order are realized in a different way — they must be understood and rationally accepted. *And this understanding and rational acceptance of the order of nature is at the same time recognition of the right of the Creator.* Elementary justice on the part of man toward God is founded on it. Man is just toward God the Creator when he recognizes the order of nature and conforms to it in his actions.[6]

In his 1968 encyclical *Humanae Vitae* (Of Human Life), Pope Paul VI frequently stressed the importance of following the biological laws, and their connection to the natural moral law.[7] We are told to "consider biological processes first," that "the teachings based on the natural law must be obeyed," and to "observe the laws inscribed on [our] nature by the Most High God" (n. 10, 11, 31).

Pope John Paul II reminded us three times in *Evangelium Vitae* (The Gospel of Life) to follow the biological laws.[8]

* "There is a plan for life which must be respected" (n. 22).

* "We are subject . . . to biological laws" (n. 42).

* We are told to "respect the biological laws inscribed in our person" (n. 97).

Breastfeeding is one significant way for us to subject ourselves to God's biological laws, to carry out God's plan for our lives.

God's breastfeeding plan is simple. Yet this simple plan can have far-reaching effects upon the human race, offering numerous benefits for the baby, for the mother, and for society. God's plan is indeed good, and it is therefore good for us to try to follow it.

∽

An icon of Jesus Christ

Evangelium Vitae is a long document, but it's fairly easy to read. In this encyclical, Pope John Paul II teaches that each human life is sacred from conception to death and that we should serve life, especially where we encounter it at its weakest. Life is at its weakest at both ends of the spectrum — the unborn and infants at one end and the elderly and infirm at the other. "Human life finds itself most vulnerable when it enters the world and when it leaves the realm of time to embark upon eternity" (n. 44). Why should we be more concerned about babies and the elderly? Evangelium Vitae teaches that every human being is "an icon of Jesus Christ," "a sign of the living God," or "the image of God's glory" (n. 84). If our babies are icons of Jesus Christ, then wouldn't we, as parents, want to give our babies the best possible care?

One of the best choices new parents can make is for the mother to breastfeed her baby.[9] God's breastfeeding plan provides numerous benefits for mother and baby, and, amazingly, many of these benefits for both mother and baby continue for years afterward.

∞

Three key truths about breastfeeding

Research strongly suggests three key conclusions about mothering and childcare during the early months and years of life.

• *Babies should be exclusively breastfed for the first six months of life.* This applies to the medically advanced countries of North America and Europe as well as to less-developed countries. *Exclusive breastfeeding* means the baby receives only mother's milk.

• *Babies should be nursed for at least one year.* The American Academy of Pediatrics (AAP), representing the pediatricians in the United States, based this recommendation for American mothers on a thorough review of the research up to 1997. The World Health Organization (WHO) and UNICEF recommend that all babies worldwide be breastfed for at least two years. (As we will see, some benefits of breastfeeding continue to accrue in the second year of life.) While I prefer the latter recommendation, I always offer the AAP recommendation when asked, "How long should a baby be nursed?" To have many more American mothers nursing their babies for at least one year would be a great improvement over the current situation.

• *A mother's consistent and loving care for her baby during the first three years of life is most important to her child's healthy emotional development.* God in his wisdom has ensured the best care for each child through prolonged lactation. Through prolonged lactation, the child can receive exclusive breastfeeding for the first six months of life, can be nursed for at least one year or possibly more, and can be ensured the presence of his mother during most of those important early years.

This chapter will be devoted to the *physical* and *health* benefits of breastfeeding, for both mother and child. The next chapter will discuss the *emotional* benefits of breastfeeding, especially as they pertain to the child during the early years.

∞

The health benefits of breastfeeding for the baby

Simply put, breast-fed babies are healthier than babies who are not breast-fed. Breast-fed babies have fewer illnesses than babies who are not breast-fed. If a breast-fed baby gets sick, his illness is usually not as severe as the same illness in a baby who is not breast-fed. This is common knowledge among well-informed doctors, researchers, and parents.

Breast milk is "liquid gold" for any baby's health.[10] Formula will never come close to the composition of human milk. There are "thirty regulated components in formula milk and over two hundred components identified in human milk."[11]

Breast milk is a living food. It changes hour by hour, day by day, month by month. The mother's body is constantly fine-tuning her milk to meet her baby's health needs. This is most evident during illness, when the breast begins to manufacture specific antibodies to fight the infection the baby has or to prevent the infection from spreading from mother to baby. Formula, of course, remains constant and does not adapt to the baby's needs as human milk does.

Breastfeeding and Catholic Motherhood

Today, professional organizations that are concerned for children promote the benefits of breastfeeding for the baby. While these benefits are sometimes described in the daily press, the research generally appears in specialty breastfeeding journals or other health publications. Thus, most people, even if they have a vague idea that breastfeeding is best, are quite unaware of its specific benefits. In addition, many who agree that breast milk is best also have the impression, skillfully developed by the baby-food marketers, that formula is just as good.

The American Academy of Family Physicians (AAFP),[12] the AAP,[13] and the United States Breastfeeding Committee[14] name many specific health benefits for breast-fed children. (There are other sources from public-health doctors, nurses, obstetricians, and gynecologists, but they usually repeat the benefits listed by these organizations.) They have found that breastfeeding tends to reduce incidences of diarrhea, allergies, ear infections, respiratory-tract infections, urinary-tract infections, diabetes, asthma, eczema, bacterial meningitis, lymphomas, childhood leukemia, inflammatory bowel disease, multiple sclerosis, sudden infant death syndrome, botulism, necrotizing enterocolitis, gastroenteritis, Hodgkin's disease, Crohn's disease, ulcerative colitis, autoimmune thyroid disease, and many other health problems large and small — including obesity in childhood and adolescence. Breast-fed babies even go on to have fewer cavities and less orthodontic work.

The health benefits of breastfeeding translate into practical lifestyle benefits, too. The same authorities also find that breast-fed children, compared with those who are not breast-fed, tend to:

- Score higher on cognitive and IQ tests in school;

- Score higher on visual acuity tests;

- Stay in the hospital fewer days as premature infants;

+ Have a more mature infant intestinal tract;

+ Have a stronger immune system;

+ Show a better response to vaccinations.

According to the AAFP, "The strongest evidence indicates that these positive effects of breastfeeding are most significant with six months of exclusive breastfeeding" and that "the effects are dose-related, with improved outcomes being associated with more, longer breastfeeding."[15]

Is formula just as good? No.

Every year in the United States, parents, insurance companies, governments, and hospitals spend up to $7 billion on conditions and diseases that might have been prevented or lessened in severity if the mother had breastfed.[16] It's estimated that universal breastfeeding in the United States would reduce health costs by approximately $1.2 billion, simply due to the reduction of insulin-dependent diabetes mellitus alone.[17] For another example, exclusively breast-fed infants have been found six to ten times less likely than formula-fed infants to develop necrotizing enterocolitis, which can cost in excess of $200,000 per case to treat.[18] Most important, some 1.5 million babies worldwide would not die each year if all mothers breastfed exclusively for six months.[19] Given such data, it is fitting to consider breastfeeding as an integral part of a pro-life mind set.

∞

More health research to support breastfeeding

Cases of acute lymphocytic leukemia, Hodgkin's lymphoma, and non-Hodgkin's lymphoma were studied from 1983 to 1997, and the results were published in 2001. Those babies who were breastfed for less than six months had almost three times more lymphoid malignancies compared with those babies breastfed for more than six months, 279 as compared with 100 cases. The researchers concluded, "The protective effect of longer breastfeeding against childhood leukemia and lymphomas is now more firmly established."[20]

A British study published in September 2002 found that total cholesterol and lipoprotein cholesterol were high in breast-fed infants, but that these levels were lower than average when those infants reached adulthood. The conclusion was that breastfeeding provided long-term benefits for cardiovascular health.[21]

Studies published in 2003 indicate that breast milk is a possible protection against Attention Deficit Hyperactivity Disorder[22] and that a high frequency of breastfeeding might reduce the risk of rheumatoid arthritis for the baby as an adult.[23]

The intelligence- and learning-related benefits of breastfeeding have also been well documented. Premature babies who had received only human milk at the hospital after birth later showed an 8.3 percent advantage in IQ over premature babies who had received other milk at the hospital.[24] Children who were breastfed for eight months or longer did better academically all the way through twelfth grade compared with children who were not breastfed.[25] A study of more than three thousand adults found that there is "a robust association between the duration of breastfeeding and adult intelligence."[26] That adults can enjoy this benefit of breastfeeding twenty to thirty years later is astounding. For parents who want their children to get As or Bs in school, choosing to breastfeed could give them an important head start.

Breastfeeding can also help prevent obesity, a health problem that has worsened recently in our nation and that contributes to an increase in the incidence of other diseases. You can't go a week without reading or hearing about this concern from the media or from teachers. Yet a 2004 study involving more than 246,000 low-income children born in seven states confirmed the fact that "breastfeeding is protective against pediatric overweight." Some of the conclusions of this research should interest every parent: "The rate of overweight at four years of age was highest among children who were never breastfed or who were breastfed for less than one month; furthermore, overweight decreased with increased breastfeeding duration. The rate of underweight was highest among children *who were never breastfed. Thus, children who were breastfed are less likely to be either overweight or underweight*" (italics mine). The researchers concluded as a result of their study that breast-feeding should be recommended for at least a year.[27]

Of course, breast-fed babies become ill, too. But statistically, babies are generally healthier and brighter when breastfed. And the advantages are more evident with a longer duration of breastfeeding.

In the beginning of the book of Daniel, Daniel and his three companions refused to eat the rich foods and wines of the king. Daniel made arrangements with the head steward that the four young men would eat only vegetables and drink only water for ten days as a test period. At the end of the ten days, Daniel and the three young men "were better in appearance and fatter than all the youths who ate the king's rich food" (Dan. 1:15). This same kind of story is being played out today. Catholic mothers choosing to breastfeed will have healthier babies than those babies raised by secular standards of bottles and babysitters.

∽

Health benefits for the mother
Mothers, too, enjoy health benefits from breastfeeding. Mothers who breastfeed their children reduce their risk of developing osteoporosis later in life, because the mother's bone growth is

stimulated as soon as weaning occurs.[28] Perhaps for similar reasons, mothers who have breastfed will have a reduction in hip fractures after menopause.[29]

Further, women who have breastfed show a reduction in ovarian-cancer rates.[30] The medical community sometimes promotes the idea that women should use artificial hormone medication to have only four periods a year — linking reduced ovulation to reduced chances of acquiring ovarian cancer. But women who breastfeed frequently enough to inhibit their menstrual cycles, and thus do not ovulate for an extended period, also reduce their risk of acquiring ovarian cancer. In the latter case, the reduction of this disease is done naturally through breastfeeding, without any medication.

Women who have breastfed their babies for an extended period have a greatly reduced risk of getting breast cancer. The researchers of a 2002 study involving more than 147,000 women concluded:

- "The relative risk of breast cancer decreased by 4.3 percent for every twelve months of breastfeeding in addition to a decrease of 7 percent for each birth."

- Women in the United States could reduce their breast cancer rate by 42 percent "solely by the longer duration of breastfeeding."

- "If women in developed countries had 2.5 children, on average, but breastfed each child for six months longer than they currently do, about 25,000 breast cancers would be prevented each year, and if each child were breastfed for an additional twelve months, about 50,000 breast cancers might be prevented annually."[31]

These researchers also said that a major contributor to the high incidence of breast cancer in our country is the fact that mothers do not breastfeed or breastfeed for only a short period. Mothers who have breastfed have a lower rate of lupus and thyroid cancer,[32] as well as of anemia and endometrial cancer.[33] Thus, prolonged lactation clearly offers special health benefits to the mother.

At the annual meeting of the American College of Rheumatology in New Orleans on October 29, 2002, Dr. Elizabeth W. Karlson of Brigham and Women's Hospital in Boston reported that women who breastfed for a total of two years or more were fifty percent less likely to develop rheumatoid arthritis than those women who breastfed for three months or less. Those who breastfed for one to two years also had a lower risk of developing rheumatoid arthritis, but the risk was the lowest among those women who breastfed for two years or more. The longer the breastfeeding, according to Dr. Karlson, the better the protection against this disease.

Thus, research shows that women who breastfeed are at a lower risk for hip fractures, ovarian cancer, breast cancer, lupus, thyroid cancer, anemia, endometrial cancer, and rheumatoid arthritis. And most of these benefits show up many years after breastfeeding.

∞

Breastfeeding, the health standard

Today there is more and more research supporting the benefits of extended breastfeeding. Breastfeeding is a health issue for both mother and baby. Breastfeeding and bottle-feeding should no longer be considered equal options, such as whether to eat peas or corn with dinner. Similar to the decision not to smoke or the decision to use seat belts when driving, the decision to breastfeed is simply more healthful than the decision to use formula.

Breastfeeding and Catholic Motherhood

The best decision is to provide your baby directly with breast milk. The next best option is to store expressed milk for when you cannot be there to feed your baby. Working mothers often use this method. The third option is to use breast milk donated by other nursing mothers and stored at a milk bank. This milk is often used by very sick or allergic babies and sometimes by very sick adults. Using formula or artificial milk is only the fourth-best option, although it is the most common nourishment given to babies in our country. Formula is convenient; we should be grateful for the availability of formula in situations when a mother truly cannot breastfeed. But the exception shouldn't replace the norm.

∞

Breastfeeding is the very best of care

If you want to give your baby the best possible chance for good health and development, then breastfeed your baby. You will enhance your own health, too. Breastfeeding is a commitment of time and sacrifice on the part of both parents. As you have seen, the Author of Nature generously rewards those mothers who make that commitment.

In the encyclical *Evangelium Vitae*, we are told seven times that "the family is the sanctuary of life."[34] The family begins with the birth of a baby, and soon the baby is at the breast of the mother.[35] The first pro-life activity new parents can do after the birth of their baby is to love and hold their baby and to breastfeed. Each baby's sanctuary should begin lovingly in the arms and at the breasts of his mother and also in the arms of his father. Remember, each and every baby is "an icon of Jesus Christ."

Chapter Two

∞

Heroic Motherhood

A mother's care during the early years of a child's life is not only important, but is crucial for that child's optimal development. Unfortunately, this topic does not get enough treatment in our society. Usually women are told they can have it all at once: motherhood *and* a career outside the home. That was what our all-female dental-hygiene class was told just before we graduated from the University of California in 1962. In fact, we were told that we *owed* it to society to continue working after we had children because of the amount of money that the state contributed toward our education.

Thus, the pressure to leave our children behind was present even back in the Sixties.

Another true story: An older woman, knowing of my interest in breastfeeding, told me that her daughter-in-law was thirty-nine and was nursing her first baby.

My reply was, "That's wonderful!"

Then the woman said, "But she went back to work, and her baby won't take a bottle."

I replied, "You said she was thirty-nine and that this is her first baby. I'm assuming she didn't *have* to go back to work."

She said, "That's right. But she's a grade-school teacher, and she misses her children."

"But her baby misses *her*," I said.

Breastfeeding and Catholic Motherhood

∞

Full-time mothering
gives babies the best start

Pope John Paul II in *Evangelium Vitae* calls mothers who dedicate themselves to the daily task of raising their children "brave mothers" and "heroic mothers." Their "daily heroism" is an ongoing sacrifice whereby they try "to pass on the best of themselves" (n. 86). There are many mothers — I had one — who felt strongly about the value of being there for their children on a regular day-to-day basis. There are many mothers today who have that same belief. I know many couples who have made sacrifices so that the mother could be there during the early years, and there are plenty of moms and dads who have made sacrifices to be available when the children are home during the school years as well.

Our top priority as parents is to raise our children as best we can. Raising children in the Lord is the most important work we do as parents. All of us want to raise children who are emotionally, spiritually, and physically healthy.

When you raise a building, you need a foundation. Our children also need a foundation. Their foundation is the first three years of life. Our job is not over after childbirth or after a child's third birthday, of course, but experts tell us that what a mother and father do during those early years is especially important in giving their children a healthy start.

Research shows that when a baby is stressed or experiences severe maternal deprivation, his brain is coated with a large dose of cortisol, a steroid hormone produced by the adrenal cortex under stress. (It is sometimes called a "stress hormone.") Abnormal levels of cortisol can be very harmful to the baby, shrinking the learning center of the brain and causing the dendrites of the nerve cells in the brain to atrophy. This helps to explain why cortisol is associated with severely delayed development. You may have seen, on television, orphaned Romanian or Russian babies rocking in their cribs, or teens moving constantly in what is called the "dance of neglect." This was caused by early maternal deprivation with its flood of cortisol.

The good news is that, by her very presence, the mother guards her baby against these harmful effects. Babies placed under stress by new or difficult situations are better protected from this stress hormone when in the arms of their mothers. Babies thrive on maternal intimacy. Breastfeeding helps provide the baby with this protection and intimacy around the clock.

What the experts are saying is that if we want caring children who will also become caring adults, they need good nurturing during the first three years of life. I do not want to rule out the exceptions, the wonderful conversions that sometimes occur, but by and large, the treatment children receive in their first three years has a great effect on their later years. Parents today are told to read often to their little ones, to hold them a lot, to love them a lot, and to talk to them frequently while making lots of eye-to-eye contact.

I want to share with you some of the work that supports the conviction that what happens in the early years is crucial for a child's development, for better or for worse.

∞

A fruitful year of parenting research

From the spring of 1997 to the spring of 1998 there was an incredible amount of research published regarding infant care. As a result of this research *Newsweek* published a 1997 issue in which the entire magazine was devoted to the "critical first three years of life." (Some of this research is included in a booklet I wrote titled

The Crucial First Three Years.[36]) All the research during that year showed two things: the importance of a consistent caregiver and the importance of breast milk. Needless to say, prolonged breast-feeding as God intended for mother and baby already provides both the consistent caregiver and the breast milk for the baby. God's plan is so good!

∞

"Fall in love with your baby"

Canadian psychiatrist Elliott Barker worked with three hundred of the most dangerous persons in Ontario at a maximum-security prison. All of these prisoners were criminally insane. Through his studies, Barker gradually became convinced that a tendency to criminal behavior can be traced back to the lack of care a person receives during the first three years of life. The greatest cruelty that can happen to human persons during the first three years, Barker said, is "to harm them so emotionally that they can never form an affectionate relationship with another human being, that they can never trust another person, and that they can never have the capacity for empathy."[37] It is during these early years that a person develops the capacity to trust, to empathize, and to show affection.

In an effort to prevent or reduce criminal activity, Barker developed a video with two presentations, *The Greatest Cruelty* and *I Don't Feel No Love*,[38] geared for seventh- to ninth-graders. In this video, the doctor tells teenagers that the most important job they will ever do is to raise their children. The job of parenting takes priority over their career and everything else, and the time during pregnancy and during the first three years are the most important years of formation. That is when the life-foundation is set. In his video, Barker tells teens to do three things as parents:

• The couple should fall in love with their baby through a positive birth experience. The father should be present at the birth.

• The mother should strengthen that love by breastfeeding her baby until he no longer needs it.

• The mother should keep her baby with her as much as possible. Separations and changing caregivers make it harder for babies to learn trust.

Dr. Barker's video is an excellent resource to promote the importance of the early years to teenagers and to young married couples. The Canadian high school teacher who introduced me to this video used it to promote breastfeeding and good parenting in his high school classes.

∽

Available, responsive, and sensitive

I have read a lot of books on child care since the Sixties. Although many of the books tell a parent how to take care of a baby, it is rare for a book to define good mothering. Have you ever thought how you would define good mothering?

In defining what a good mother does, the book I found most helpful was William Gairdner's *The War Against the Family*.[39] In it, Gairdner defines the "good" mother by the kind of care she gives her little one. He asks himself, "How do we avoid sociopaths?" More positively, a parent might ask, "How do I raise emotionally healthy children?" Gairdner's answer centers on the kind of care the mother gave her child during the early years.

According to Gairdner, a mother should be available, she should respond to her baby, and she should respond in a sensitive manner.[40] In other words, a good mother has these qualities: Availability, Responsiveness, and Sensitivity, or ARS. Based on the work of researchers at three major universities, Gairdner claims that ARS care has been consistently shown to be necessary to meet the real needs of babies.

With breastfeeding, a mother learns to be available because she has to be there to feed her baby. By her presence, the nursing mother is in a good position to respond to her baby, and to do so in a loving and sensitive manner. The sensitivity would likely be assisted by the strong bonding and the mothering hormone present in her body due to the breastfeeding.

Gairdner further defines a good mother by what she provides: "Young children need an uninterrupted, intimate, and continuous connection with their mother, especially in the very early months and years."[41] Again, this is easy to do when a mother breastfeeds.

Mothering that includes breastfeeding is *uninterrupted*. The mother has to be there to nurse her child. The nursing baby continually needs the presence of his mother.

Breastfeeding is *intimate*. With breastfeeding there is a special physical and emotional closeness between mother and child. The baby is physically intimate with his mother, wrapped up in her arms and looking at her face on a regular basis. Babies thrive on this maternal intimacy.

Breastfeeding is *continuous*. Certainly nursing for many months is a series of events that deserves to be called continuous.

∞

The early years are
crucial for emotional health
In their 1997 book *Ghosts from the Nursery*, Robin Karr-Morse and Meredith Wiley address the problem of juvenile crime, which

had quadrupled in the previous twenty-five years. They lament the fact that, "There are more children now than ever before who are growing up without guidance, responsibility, or internalized social values."[42] Like Gairdner, they summarize the importance of the mother's being there and responding in a sensitive manner. Like Barker, they are concerned that individuals develop empathy for the other person. Karr-Morse and Wiley repeat a familiar conclusion: "The foundation for empathy is laid from the beginning when the early months of an infant's experience include consistent, sensitive interactions in which the caregiver accurately assesses the child's needs and responds quickly in a soothing manner."[43] That caregiver by nature is usually the mother.

Ken Magid, co-author of the book *High Risk: Children Without a Conscience*, is concerned about the emotional health of our children. He writes that whatever happens to a baby during the first two years of his life — good or bad — will affect that baby's life as an adult: "A complex set of events must occur in infancy to assure a future of trust and love. If the proper bonding and subsequent attachment does not occur — between the child and the mother — the child will develop mistrust and a deep-seated rage. He becomes a child without a conscience."[44]

Among Magid's answers to this potential problem is breastfeeding. Breastfeeding "is anchoring, gives a sense of security, and prevents high risk because it helps produce healthy brain development and attachment."[45] Besides breastfeeding, he also encourages parents to sway, rock, swing, and hold their baby; for "second to killing someone, [subjecting him to] isolation is the worst thing we can do."[46] Many adults experience the suffering of isolation when they are treated unjustly, feeling conflict or loneliness or persecution. Yet adults have mature brains, and they adapt. But isolation is very difficult for children.

Breastfeeding and Catholic Motherhood

I have often wondered about the early years of criminals. What were their lives like when they were innocent babies? In 2004 there were eighty-two inmates on death row nationwide, *for crimes committed when they were under eighteen.*[47] What were their early years like with their mothers? Were they breastfed? If so, for how long? What sort of intimacy did they enjoy with their mothers or fathers?

I know that not all problems will be solved by mothers staying home when their children are little. We all know of some mother who chose to stay home but wasn't good with her children, but such cases are the exception. Overall, the experts I have quoted are trying to show parents that there is a way to increase your chances of raising emotionally healthy individuals.

∽

Breastfeeding is a sign of mother's love

In Scripture we read about the good care by nursing mothers. The child is "quieted at its mother's breasts" (Ps. 131:2), is satisfied with the mother's "consoling breasts" (Isa. 66:11), is "carried upon her hip, and dandled upon her knee" while nursing (Isa. 66:12), and is safe at its "mother's breasts" (Ps. 22:9). Good mothering is depicted in Scripture through the mother who nurses and has close physical contact with her baby.

I would like to share some of the words of Maria Montessori, a pioneer who has had a tremendous impact upon our society in the area of childhood education. Wouldn't it be just as wonderful if she had a similar impact on mothers?

Maria Montessori said that prolonged breastfeeding usually lasts from one and a half years to three years; this "requires the mother to remain with her child, and this satisfies her unconscious need to give her offspring the help of a full social life on which to construct his mind."[48] She observed that babies do not cry when they remain with their mother. On the other hand, people in our society complain about the crying of their babies. She wrote:

> But let us think, for a moment, of the many peoples of the world who live at different cultural levels from our own. In the matter of child rearing, almost all of these seem to be more enlightened than ourselves — with all our Western ultramodern ideals. Nowhere else, in fact, do we find children treated in a fashion so opposed to their natural needs. In almost all countries, the baby accompanies his mother wherever she goes. Mother and baby are inseparable. All the while they are out together, mother talks and baby listens. If the mother argues about prices with a vendor, it is in the child's presence; he sees and hears all that goes on. And this lasts for the whole period of maternal feeding, which is the reason for this close alliance.
>
> For the mother has to feed her child, and therefore she cannot leave him at home when she goes out. To this need for food is added their mutual fondness and love. In this way, the child's need for nutrition, and the love that unites these two beings, both combine in solving the problem of the child's adaptation to the world, and this happens in the most natural way possible. Mother and child are one.
>
> Except where civilization has broken down this custom, no mother ever entrusts her child to someone else.[49]

Maria Montessori was a true advocate of prolonged lactation and of mother-baby inseparability. She knew that God designed female human nature so that the mother's body can provide both.

Breastfeeding and Catholic Motherhood

∞

The importance of fathers

Whenever someone speaks about the importance of mothering today, there is always someone who asks, "What about fathers? Aren't they important also?" David Blankenhorn wrote a book, *Fatherless America,* and lectures throughout the United States on the importance of fathering. He calls the father "that first significant other. The father is the first encounter with an intimate other,"[50] Here he means "other than mother," for he also stresses the importance of the mother-baby dyad during the first three years of life.

Gairdner expresses this same thought well: "An avalanche of recent 'attachment studies' has shown that although fathers are terribly important to any child's development, attachment bonding is overwhelmingly a matter of the quality and continuance of the relationship between the *mother* and her children in the early stages of life."[51]

Herbert Ratner was a public-health doctor and a convert to the Catholic Faith who gave many talks to the laity on marriage and family and who was a strong advocate of breastfeeding and good parenting. He made the following comments on fathers:

> I will give you two words that characterize what fathers have to offer their children, and these apply to parents in general. Love and time. The father "romances" each new child by delighting in and falling in love with the newborn. In addition, the male gives moral and emotional support by appreciating the nurturing mother and is customarily the provider and the protector of the mother and child. With the passage of time, he contributes more and more to the emotional, intellectual, and moral formation of the child.[52]

I believe that the father is an invaluable support for the mother's emotions as she "works" with her children. His love and support can help her feel good about herself as she devotes herself to the task of good mothering and to breastfeeding. Behind most successful breastfeeding mothers is a good husband and father who offers spiritual and emotional support to his wife, and who provides for her and their children so that she can be there to raise their children. Dads can enjoy their little ones through many activities. They can spend time with their babies by holding them, playing with them, walking them, dancing with them, bathing them, dressing them, reading to them, singing and whistling to them, teaching them, and praying in their presence. Dads today can be as involved with their children as they choose to be, forming close and intimate relationships with them by spending time with them. Any child today is especially lucky when he has two parents who love him dearly and who express that love in these simple ways.

∞

The emotional health benefits
of breastfeeding for the mother

Many mothers report being happy and emotionally satisfied with their breastfeeding. Happier mothers usually means happier babies and children.

There are two mothering hormones, oxytocin and prolactin, that are present in the mother's body when she breastfeeds. These hormones help the mother to relax and enjoy her baby. The following quotation, from a mother I know, typifies the widespread experience of nursing your baby: "I experience true feelings of euphoria when nursing. All the worries and cares of the world quickly vanish as soon as my baby is at my breast."

Breastfeeding and Catholic Motherhood

Mothering hormones might be one reason mothers learn to relax and enjoy their baby and helps explain the closeness that mothers feel as they breastfeed. Many mothers I have known say that breastfeeding has made them better, more patient parents. One friend confided to me that she would lose her patience and spank her non-breast-fed baby now and then. With her next, breast-fed baby, she stopped spanking. She felt the change in her behavior was due to that special bond she had with this child because of breastfeeding.

I know breastfeeding made me a better mother. It kept me focused on the most important gifts in my marriage: my children. If I had bottle-fed my babies, I'm sure I would have felt unneeded, gotten lazy, and let the children feed themselves with a bottle as soon as possible. I probably would not have sat down, placed them in my lap, and fed them with the bottle every time they were hungry, as I did with breastfeeding. I would have missed out on countless hours of intimate bonding spent in close proximity to my little ones.

Breastfeeding is a win-win situation. It's not only best for the baby, but it's best for the mother. Breastfeeding teaches a mother that she is important and needed. A nursing mother can't ignore the hungry baby or let the little one feed himself. She has to participate in the feeding of her child. Breastfeeding teaches the mother to be a good mother in a natural way.

If every mother breastfed her baby, mothers and children would be healthier, both physically and emotionally, and our society would be healthier. Any mother can do the ordinary thing, breastfeed, in order to give her child the best possible care. There is nothing extraordinary here, just a simple plan:

• She can breastfeed until the child no longer needs it.

• She can avoid separations with her baby.

• She can be available to her child and respond to him in a sensitive manner.

• She can allow her young children to have that uninterrupted, intimate, and continuous connection with her during the first three years of life.

∞

Mothers are irreplaceable

As I mentioned earlier, in *Evangelium Vitae*, John Paul II referred to mothers as "brave" and "heroic" because they do not receive much support from the world. Mothers who choose to stay with their children during the early years need support from friends, relatives, and the Church. In our society, unfortunately, the mother who leaves her children is often applauded, while the mother who remains home usually receives little encouragement. The trend today is to leave the care of our children to others, oftentimes strangers. More than half of the children under two years of age are cared for by someone other than their parents for some time each day.[53] Of course, I realize there are many mothers who would prefer to be with their children but for various reasons are unable to do so. These mothers deserve our support, too!

Pope John Paul II has spoken strongly about the importance of the role the mother plays in society. At the beatification of Sister Marijz Petkovic in June 2003, the Pope spoke of the importance of women as wives and mothers and noted that all women have a special role as nurturers. "In a special way, God has entrusted children to your care, and thus you are called to become an important support in the life of every person, especially within the context of the family."[54] Similarly, in his 1981 encyclical *On Human Work*, John Paul II wrote:

It will redound to the credit of society to make it possible for a mother — without inhibiting her freedom, without psychological or practical discrimination, and without penalizing her as compared with other women — to devote herself to taking care of her children and educating them in accordance with their needs, which vary with age.

Having to abandon these tasks in order to take up paid work outside the home is wrong from the point of view of the good of society and of the family when it contradicts or hinders these primary goals of a mother (n. 47).

Most important, in this same encyclical, John Paul II says that mothers are irreplaceable.

The *true advancement of women* requires that labor should be structured in such a way that women do not have to pay for their advancement by abandoning what is specific to them and at the expense of the family, in which the women as mothers have an irreplaceable role (n. 47).

In his address at the Eleventh General Assembly of the Pontifical Council for the Family in 1994, John Paul II said that "women can never be replaced in begetting and rearing children" and that "the woman has a right to the honor and joy of motherhood."[55] The Pope said that the "woman's main role as wife and mother is to place her in the heart of the family; her irreplaceable role must be appreciated and recognized."[56]

What about the children? Do they have any rights? Yes! According to John Paul II, "Children have the right to the care and concern of those who have begotten them, their mothers in particular."[57] In other words, the baby has the right to be cared for, with love, by his mother.

Years earlier, Pope Pius XII stressed the importance of mother-hood, saying that "mothers . . . exert the earliest and the most inti-mate influence upon the souls of little ones and upon their growth in piety and virtue. . . . No art is more difficult and strenuous than that of fashioning the souls of children."[58] The first education be-gins in the early years with the mother. Pius XII tells mothers to "keep a vigilant eye upon your babies throughout their infancy, watching over their growth and over the health of their little bod-ies, for this is flesh of your flesh and the fruit of your womb."[59] The mother feeds this baby's body and soul "with breast and smile."[60] Regarding the task of Christian mothers, "none can fully take their place."[61]

∽

"I'm needed at home"

I began this chapter with a story and would like to end it in the same way.

In April 2002, I gave a luncheon address on the various chal-lenges a woman faces if she chooses to stay home with her chil-dren. When I returned to my table, a professional woman said to me, "That's where I was. I was one of those women who went back to work after childbirth. I enjoyed my work and never wanted to be home. But every now and then, something would happen that would tell me maybe my choice was not the right one.

"For example, one time my little girl drew a picture of our fam-ily. Dad's car was in the driveway. Only she and dad were in the picture. I asked, 'Where's Mommy?' My little girl said, 'You know you're never home, Mommy.'

"Then, at a staff meeting, my boss introduced a new employ-ment option. Without a reduction in salary, we could choose to work the entire weekend, Saturday and Sunday, and not work at all Monday through Friday. I decided to take it. I told my supervisor, 'I'm needed at home.' "

The next time her little girl drew a picture of her family, she drew *all* the family members — but this time, Mom was three times bigger than everyone else. The woman immediately showed her husband, bragging, "Look how big I am now!" She was a happy mother. She also had a happier daughter.

Mothers who breastfeed are indeed heroic.[62] It is through the many acts of breastfeeding that a woman soon experiences how truly irreplaceable she is!

Chapter Three

⧜

Church Teaching on Breastfeeding

What, if anything, does the Catholic Church teach about breast-feeding? Father William Virtue, a priest from the Diocese of Peoria, Illinois, asked this very question in the early 1990s. His search for answers culminated in the publication of his book, *Mother and Infant*, in 1995.[63] From his research, Father Virtue concluded that "the testimony of the Magisterium [the official teaching authority of the Church] and moral experts confirms that it has been the constant teaching of the Church that there is a serious obligation of maternal nursing."[64] Father Virtue argues that breastfeeding is a "duty of good mothering," being "the optimal way to nurture the physical and emotional-relational dimensions of the human infant."[65]

The child, he says, has a right to his mother's milk, and the mother has a duty to provide it. Father Virtue further believes that this serious obligation is also based on "the moral value of maternal nursing as forming the infant in love" due to the psychological benefits of breastfeeding.[66]

By "serious obligation," Father Virtue doesn't mean that failure to breastfeed is a mortal sin, but that the choice to breastfeed is a real duty that cannot be ignored for trivial reasons.[67] Parents have a general obligation to do what is best for their children, within their abilities and means. I think good parents recognize that duty and really want to do what is best for their babies. Father

Breastfeeding and Catholic Motherhood

Virtue believes that because breastfeeding is God's own plan for baby care and since it is so economical (and thus within almost everyone's means), this ordinarily translates into an obligation to breastfeed.

∽

Great papal support for breastfeeding

In his book, Father Virtue lists a few popes and saints who have supported breastfeeding, including Pope Gregory the Great, Pope Benedict XIV, St. Clement, St. Basil, St. Ambrose, and St. John Chrysostom.[68] In more recent times, both Pope Pius XII and Pope John Paul II have promoted breastfeeding. On October 26, 1941, Pope Pius XII took time out from his busy wartime schedule to address an association of Italian mothers. He reminded them that the mother's influence and her education of the soul and body of her infant begin at the cradle. He urged all mothers to breastfeed their babies, if at all possible.

> We see in mothers those who exert the earliest and the most intimate influence upon the souls of the little ones and upon their growth in piety and virtue.
>
> Surely there is no art more difficult and strenuous than that of fashioning the souls of children; for those souls are so very tender, so easily disfigured through some thoughtless influence or wrong advice, so difficult to guide aright and so lightly led astray.
>
> This is the reason why, except where it is quite impossible, it is more desirable that the mother should feed her child at her own breast. Who shall say what mysterious influences are exerted upon the growth of that little creature by the mother upon whom it depends entirely for its development.[69]

On March 18, 1994, John Paul II spoke to Nafis Sadik, then executive director of the United Nations Fund for Population Activities, and he criticized the final draft document for the up-coming September meeting of the United Nations International Conference on Population and Development in Cairo, Egypt. To my knowledge, this is the only time John Paul II has talked publicly about the child-spacing effects of breastfeeding. Here is part of his talk:

> Greater consideration should be given to the social role of mothers, and support be given to programs which aim at decreasing maternal mortality, providing prenatal and perinatal care, meeting the nutritional needs of pregnant women and nursing mothers themselves to provide preventive health care for their infants. In this regard, attention should be given to the positive benefits of breastfeeding for nourishment and disease prevention in infants, as well as for maternal bonding and birth spacing.[70]

On May 12, 1995, Pope John Paul II met with participants in a study session on "Breastfeeding: Science and Society" sponsored by the Pontifical Academy of Sciences and the Royal Society of Great Britain. The Pope spoke of the social presupposition that it is perfectly acceptable for a mother to leave her baby, and of the need to set policy to support the mothers who care for their children. "Even this brief reflection on the very individual and private act of a mother feeding her infant," he said, "can lead us to a deep and far-ranging critical rethinking of certain social and economic presuppositions, the negative human and moral consequences of which are becoming more and more difficult to ignore."

In his address to scientists, he spoke of the advantages of breast-feeding. The Pope's comments make it clear that he understands the seriousness of this issue and is quite knowledgeable about the current state of affairs as it pertains to the practice of breastfeeding. Here is the main body of the Pope's talk, in which he endorses the 1990 UNICEF recommendation of exclusive breastfeeding for four to six months, and to nurse "up to the second year of life or beyond":

As scientists, you direct your enquiry toward a better understanding of the advantages of breastfeeding for the infant and the mother. In normal circumstances, these include two major benefits to the child: protection against disease and proper nourishment. Moreover, in addition to these immunological and nutritional effects, this natural way of feeding can create a bond of love and security between mother and child, and enable the child to assert its *presence as a person* through interaction with the mother.

All of this is obviously a matter of immediate concern to countless women and children, and something that clearly has general importance for every society, rich or poor. One hopes that your studies will serve to *heighten public awareness of how much this natural activity benefits the child and helps to create the closeness and maternal bonding* so necessary for healthy child development. So human and natural is this bond that the Psalms use the image of the infant at its mother's breast as a picture of God's care for man (cf. Ps 22:9). So vital is this interaction between mother and child that my predecessor Pope Pius XII urged Catholic mothers, if at all possible, to nourish their children themselves (cf. *Allocution to Mothers,* 26 October 1941).

From various perspectives, therefore, the theme is of interest to the Church, called as she is to concern herself with the sanctity of life and of the family.

Worldwide surveys indicate that *two-thirds of mothers still breastfeed,* at least to some extent. But statistics also show that there has been a fall in the number of women who nourish their infants in this way, not only in developed countries where the practice almost has to be reinstituted, but also increasingly in developing countries. This decline is traced to a combination of social factors such as urbanization and the increasing demands placed on women, to health-care policies and practices, and to marketing strategies for alternate forms of nourishment.

Yet the overwhelming body of research is in favor of natural feeding rather than its substitutes. Responsible international agencies are calling on governments to ensure that women are enabled to breastfeed their children for four to six months from birth and to continue this practice, supplemented by other appropriate foods, up to the second year of life or beyond (cf. UNICEF, Children and Development in the 1990s on the occasion of the World Summit for Children, New York, 29-30 September 1990). Your meeting, therefore, intends to illustrate the scientific bases for encouraging social policies and employment conditions which allow mothers to do this.

In practical terms, what we are saying is that *mothers need time, information, and support.*

So much is expected of women in many societies that time to devote to breastfeeding and early care is not always available. Unlike other modes of feeding, no one can substitute for the mother in this natural activity. Likewise, women have a right to be informed truthfully about the advantages of this practice, as also about the difficulties involved in some cases. Health-care professionals, too, should be encouraged and properly trained to help women in these matters.[71]

When I was breastfeeding in the 1960s to the 1980s, there was little official support from the Church. In fact, when I wrote the first edition of *Breastfeeding and Natural Child Spacing* in 1969, the editor of my home archdiocesan newspaper refused to accept my ad, saying that he did not want the word *breastfeeding* in the newspaper!

We have come a long way since then. The research concerning breastfeeding is ample today. Father Virtue and others have made a strong case that Church teaching encourages mothers to breast-feed. The endorsements of Pope Pius XII and Pope John Paul II have been blessings.

∾

Bishops and other Church
leaders advocate breastfeeding

Another churchman who was well known for his support of breastfeeding was the late Bishop James T. McHugh, who intro-duced the Holy Father at the Vatican breastfeeding conference in 1995. In his introductory remarks, he talked about societal pres-sures that tend to discourage breastfeeding.

There is considerable evidence that breastfeeding provides proper nutrition for children and also protects the child against life-threatening infections in the earliest years of life. The mother also benefits by knowing that she is pro-viding good nourishment, and research shows that breast-feeding is associated with a reduction in the risk of breast cancer. The return of ovulation is inhibited in the fully breastfeeding women, at least during the first six months after birth, thereby providing important health benefits to the family because of improved birth spacing.

Unfortunately there are many factors that discourage or inhibit women from this important practice. In developed countries, the rapid pace of life and time demands on women are obstacles. Absence of stable family life and familial support affects many women. Employment patterns, the work environment, and the absence of sufficient maternal leave-time create difficulties.

In developing countries where breastfeeding has been a more common practice, urbanization, work outside the home, and other aspects of modernization tend to diminish the practice of breastfeeding. It is important to protect and strengthen the cultural support for breastfeeding practices within the family.[72]

In the summer of 1998, Alfonso Cardinal López Trujillo, President of the Pontifical Council for the Family, volunteered to write the foreword for my book *Breastfeeding and Natural Child Spacing*. In the foreword, he encouraged couples to "remain open to God's gift of new life" and noted that many couples are not aware of the natural spacing of births through breastfeeding. Cardinal López Trujillo stressed the closeness between mother and child and the many health benefits of breastfeeding. He also wrote:

As one of the natural ways for regulating fertility, breastfeeding thus takes its place among various methods that constitute the "authentic alternative" to contraception, and so it remains a subject for research and study. . . . As they [husband and wife] serve the divine plan and cooperate with the Creator, the natural benefits of the cycles and processes that God provides are soon evident. These benefits are particularly obvious in the nurturing and nourishing of breastfeeding.

Here we have a tangible example of the positive value of the natural way of transmitting human life.[73]

∽

Support from the grassroots

Church support for breastfeeding comes not only from popes and bishops, but also from everyday parish priests and ministers. Father Jerry Hiland of Cincinnati felt called by the Holy Spirit to deliver a homily on breastfeeding at one Sunday Mass. The responses were very positive. As one parishioner said, "Father made me feel so good about the fact that I had breastfed our children. My children had done very well scholastically, and Father made me realize that I might have had some part to play in that" — referring to the role breastfeeding plays in a child's cognitive development.

Occasionally a priest will write an article about Natural Family Planning and devote some attention to breastfeeding. Father William Saunders, dean of the Notre Dame Graduate School of Christendom College in Virginia, wrote an article for the *Arlington Catholic Herald* on July 20, 2000, in which he said:

One of the earliest forms of Natural Family Planning is breastfeeding. If a woman breastfeeds her baby consistently, she probably will not conceive for eighteen to twenty-four months. Actually, many tribal people naturally regulate births this way.

In April 2002, I corresponded with a nun from the Sisters of Life, a strong advocate of breastfeeding who knows the importance of the first three years of life for healthy child development. She works with pregnant women in crisis and new single mothers in the New York area. In a letter to me, she wrote, "I'm finding many opportunities to share this information with others as our works are constantly bringing us in touch with those for whom these topics are relevant to their lives or work."

An increasing number of Catholic communities and parishes are supporting breastfeeding mothers. Father Al Lauer began Presentation Ministries in the Cincinnati area in 1983. This diocesan priest encouraged home-based communities and was a strong promoter of breastfeeding. Today those who associate with Presentation Ministries soon learn that breastfeeding babies, no matter what their age, are always welcome at community Mass, retreats, meetings, or social gatherings of any kind.

Father Lauer's recent writings in *One Bread, One Body* reminded me of his support for breastfeeding:

> Only a woman can conceive a human being, give birth to her child, and nurture her child at the breast. Because the spiritual is based on the natural (1 Cor. 15:46), this indicates the heart of femininity as life-bearer and nurturer. Only the Holy Spirit can guide us to understand and develop this rightly.
>
> Even with these initial insights into true masculinity and femininity, it obviously takes courage to be ourselves. Leadership requires sacrifice and the willingness to be rejected. It takes courage to lead. In an abortifacient, contraceptive culture, how courageous women are to conceive, birth, and nurture human life! Take courage and be yourself.[74]

Working to develop a Marian spirituality based on Mother Mary's nursing, Father Timothy Sauppé of Illinois wrote that Mary is "in her most womanly and politically incorrect role when she is maternally breastfeeding the Child Jesus."[75] This priest turned a former office room into a Madonna Chapel featuring religious art-work of Mary nursing Jesus. Father Sauppé hopes his educational materials in the chapel will encourage women to have more chil-dren and to breastfeed.

Father Sauppé also created a new Mother of God chaplet to re-flect the five divine mysteries of Mary's Maternity (see Appendix). This priest travels regularly to other parishes to promote breast-feeding and the "Madonna Chapel."

∞

Catholics can still do more

Despite the Church's strong official and growing grassroots support of breastfeeding, there is much more that can be done. Church leaders can encourage the oneness of the mother-baby relationship associated with breastfeeding by making mothers feel comfortable nursing modestly at Mass or at church and school functions. Educate your pastors about breastfeeding, and encour-age them to take a positive, tolerant view of modest nursing in church.

Catholic mothers and Catholic couples can also play an impor-tant role in offering encouragement and example at the parish level or in society. Anyone — priest, nun, or layperson — can compliment a mother or couple upon learning their baby is breast-fed. It takes only a few words of encouragement to make the woman or the couple feel good about their choice to breastfeed their baby.

If a couple has a strong obligation to try to breastfeed their baby due to its many benefits and out of respect for God's plan for life, does not the Church likewise have an obligation to promote breastfeeding? Letters I have received indicate that many Catho-lics, as well as couples of other faiths, have avoided the use of contraceptive practices because of the mother's extended breast-feeding infertility. Breastfeeding can lead to conversions. Some couples claim that their first step toward conversion to the Catholic Faith was reading my book *Breastfeeding and Natural Child Spacing*, which led them to accept Natural Family Planning.

Father James Otto of Philadelphia once stated a simple truth about the good influence of the clergy: "One layperson can say something, and it may have little impact. But a priest can say the same thing, and it has the impact of a thousand laypersons saying it." The Church's educational system is unique, beginning with the parents prior to their baby's Baptism, through grade school, high school, and college, through marriage preparation — not to mention retreats, conferences, and parish programs.[76] A few sentences on breastfeeding at the appropriate time by those representing the Church, especially priests and nuns, can have a strong influence among the laity.

The encouragement of breastfeeding by the Church need not stop with John Paul II or with Father William Virtue. As they learn the full truth, there is real hope that those teaching about life, love, and family within the Church will increasingly teach this beautiful part of God's plan for mothers and their babies.

Chapter Four

Breastfeeding:
A Continuation of Pregnancy

When you consider the close protective care of the baby by the mother during pregnancy and breastfeeding, you begin to see that breastfeeding is truly a continuation of pregnancy. After child-birth, the baby has merely switched positions from the womb to the breasts and arms of the mother. The breasts, in essence, have replaced the placenta.[77]

Certain physical conditions that are present during pregnancy continue to exist for the baby and the mother during breastfeeding. For example:

• *During pregnancy, the mother's body provides exclusive nourishment for her baby.* During the early months of exclusive breastfeeding, the mother's body continues to provide exclusive nourishment. The nourishment provided by the placenta for the unborn baby in the womb is replaced after childbirth by the nourishment at the breasts. The baby continues to grow and thrive at the breast, receiving breast milk alone for his nourishment, just as the baby grew and thrived in the mother's womb.

The mother's body can meet the nutritional needs of her baby for fifteen to seventeen months (combining the time of pregnancy and the early months of breastfeeding). After six to eight months of exclusive breastfeeding, the nursing baby will need other foods to supplement his mother's milk. Even with supplementation, breast milk will be a source of nutrition for many young children up to and even beyond their second birthdays.

• *The physical oneness of mother and baby during pregnancy continues with the oneness of mother and baby during breastfeeding.* During pregnancy, the mother's body provides much-needed touch and close physical contact with her baby. The mother's body continues to provide this intimate touch and close physical contact through breastfeeding.

With pregnancy, the baby thrives both emotionally and physically in a very close "motherly" environment. Babies also thrive on the maternal intimacy they receive with breastfeeding. The security of the womb is replaced at birth with the security of the mother's breasts and arms and overall physical closeness of her body. The mother who nurses her baby provides close physical intimacy on a routine basis. Breastfeeding provides a constant and intimate environment in which almost all babies thrive emotionally and physically.

The norm is mother-baby togetherness. As the World Health Organization so appropriately stated, "Mothers and babies form an inseparable biological and social unit; the health and nutrition of one group cannot be divorced from the health and nutrition of the other."[78]

Robin Karr-Norse and Meredith Wiley expressed this biological oneness well in their book *Ghosts from the Nursery:*

> Nurturing behaviors such as holding, touching, making eye contact, speaking, and rocking . . . provide for the regulation of basic biological functions in the infant. These functions include the immune system, blood pressure, body temperature, appetite, sleep, and cardiovascular regulation. The

infant is so fundamentally dependent for these functions on the mother's continuous proximity that many researchers refer to the mother and baby as one biological system.[79]

• *During both pregnancy and breastfeeding, the mother usually goes many months without any menstruation.* For a nursing mother to have her menstrual cycles return within three months after childbirth should be the exception, not the norm. Mothers who nurse their babies frequently day and night, remain with their babies, and follow a form of mothering that avoids mother-baby separation and the use of pacifiers and bottles, will experience the absence of menstruation, on the average, fourteen to fifteen months after childbirth. Nature intends the typical mother to receive more months without menstruation through breastfeeding than through pregnancy. By nature's standards, it is normal for a nursing mother to go one, two, or even three years after childbirth without menstruation. (The requirements for experiencing normal breastfeeding infertility are covered in chapter 6.)

Breastfeeding was God's own plan for spacing babies since the beginning of mankind. It still is. The nine months of pregnancy without any menstrual cycles followed by usually many more months of breastfeeding without menstrual cycles is a normal, natural occurrence. These two continuous events, pregnancy and breastfeeding, are part of the normal infertility "cycle" of the reproductive system. Both events keep mother and baby together biologically for a considerable period.

∽

Continuous care from pregnancy to breastfeeding
Dr. Nils Bergman from Cape Town, South Africa, is a promoter of an infant-care method called Kangaroo Mother Care. This

method involves continuous maternal skin-to-skin contact, and breastfeeding starts right after birth. Dr. Bergman wants the baby to remain on the mother's body near her breasts after birth. This recommendation, even for premature babies, is based on physiological tests and mortality rates showing that this type of care is best for the health of the baby. It is because of this mother-baby closeness after birth that Bergman, too, teaches that breastfeeding is a continuation of pregnancy.[80]

In his wonderful plan, God provides each baby with a continuity of care by his mother — from pregnancy to breastfeeding. After childbirth, God continues to provide the newborn with special care, uninterrupted care by the mother. This personal and intimate care via breastfeeding is also usually very pleasurable and rewarding for both mother and baby.

Scripture reminds us of this continuity of care with these words of a mother to her son: "I carried you nine months in my womb and nursed you for three years" (2 Macc. 7:27). This mother was conscious that her care for her son began in the womb and continued at the breast. Breastfeeding during the early months is an extension of pregnancy with regard to the total care of the mother for her baby, especially when the mother follows the natural order. Just as they were during pregnancy, mother and baby are a biological unit after childbirth, united in a loving, caring embrace.

Chapter Five

Breastfeeding and the Marriage Act

Many comparisons can be made between the marriage act and the act of breastfeeding. In pointing out such similarities, I don't mean to denigrate the sacrament of Matrimony. God established marriage from the beginning of the human race, and Christ raised marriage between two Christians to the level of a sacrament. The marriage act is of utmost importance and value; in it, a man and wife become co-creators with God in bringing children into the world. Experts who study the health of society speak about the importance of the strength and permanence of the husband-wife marital relationship as well as the importance of how parents, especially mothers, raise their young. In addition, many acts involving service or gift of self to others (such as teacher to students or priest to parishioners) also have avenues for comparison. This is an area where I hope future theologians will develop deeper thoughts concerning maternal nursing.

For the present, though, I offer eleven simple points of comparison between breastfeeding and the marriage act, in the hope of further elevating the importance of each:

- They are voluntary acts between two persons.

- Both acts are normally essential for life.

- The woman offers her body to her husband in the marriage act and to her baby in the breastfeeding act.

• Both acts in Scripture are used to describe God's love for his people.

• Both acts involve love through intimacy, physical closeness, and emotional bonding.

• Both acts normally involve physical pleasure.

• Both acts can impact the health of a family and thus society.

• Both acts ought to involve a gift of self to another.

• The Pope's theology of the body applies to both acts.

• Each act involves a love that unifies the two persons.

• Both acts have two orders, the order of nature and the personal order.

Let us consider each point:

• *Both are purely voluntary acts that bring about a communion of two persons:* the marriage act between husband and wife and the breastfeeding act between mother and child.

• *Both acts are necessary in God's plan for the continuation of the human race.* Both acts are normally essential for life. The marriage act is needed to create new persons and to help the bonding of the spouses, and the breastfeeding act is needed for the survival of those new persons and for the bonding of mother and baby. It's true that today science can create babies without the marriage act, and we can also feed babies without the mother. The latter is sometimes even necessary for the life of the baby and thus a great good. Frequently, however, it is done primarily for the convenience of the parents, and this unhappy practice has become the social custom in many cultures. Because breastfeeding is so uncommon, we tend to forget the important role it should play in feeding and nurturing infants and young children.

• *In both acts, a woman gives herself bodily:* in the marriage act, to her husband, and in the breastfeeding act, to her baby. The woman's giving to her husband should not detract from her giving to her baby. Likewise her giving to her baby or child should not detract from the love shown to her husband.

Love is not exclusive or limiting. There is no restriction. The relationship that a woman has with her husband and with her baby are obviously different, but both relationships involve giving and loving. Neither relationship should detract from the other. A good husband appreciates his wife's important role as mother in nurturing his children. In addition, breastfeeding, once established, becomes such an easy activity. The mother can converse with her husband, be affectionate, and share in his interests and activities and still be with and nurse her baby.

• *Scripture denotes God's love for his people by referring to both acts.* In the Old Testament, God's loving care for his people is compared to the loving care of a nursing mother for her child (Isa. 66: 12-13). In the New Testament, a husband's love for his wife is compared to Christ's spousal love for his Church (Eph. 5:21-33).

• *Both acts involve love through intimacy, physical closeness, and emotional bonding.* The marriage act is for babies and for bonding. Breastfeeding is also for babies and for bonding.

• *Both acts are associated with rightful pleasure.* God made both acts pleasurable and good to ensure that the race would continue. Thus husband and wife would want to come together in the marriage act, and the mother would want to stay with and nurse her baby.

Breastfeeding and Catholic Motherhood

• *Both biological acts have an impact upon the family and society.* When the two persons, husband and wife, remain together in faithful marriage, both family and society benefit. Children do much better in all facets of their lives when they have their two parents living together in the same household. We all probably know people who claim the divorce of their parents was one of the worst events in their lives.[81]

Breastfeeding likewise can have a significant impact, physically and emotionally, on the health of an individual and the family and thus upon society. As we have already seen in chapter 2, experts tell us that how a mother cares for her child during the first three years of life can have a tremendous impact upon the health of our society. God in his wisdom helps to ensure this care during most of the first three years of life through prolonged lactation.

• *Both acts should involve the gift of self to another.* Husband and wife show their intimate love for each other physically and emotionally in the marriage act, giving themselves to each other without holding anything back, including their fertility. Breastfeeding helps the mother become a "gift of self" to her baby continually throughout the day. Breastfeeding teaches a mother to put her baby first and to give of her time for the needs of her baby. This learning process occurs in an easy and natural way with breastfeeding.

A mother can be a very busy person, and bottle-feeding allows someone other than the mother to attend to the needs of the baby. Soon a "bottle baby" can feed himself. But the beauty of God's plan is that it keeps bringing the baby back to the mother frequently for food and comfort at the breast. Thus breastfeeding provides an environment in which the mother gradually learns to become a good mother, to become that gift of self to her baby.

Because we are only human, we know that there may occasionally be grumbling and complaining between husband and wife or by the breastfeeding mother over her particular situation. But in both relationships, the married couple and the breastfeeding mother should have the faithful commitment to be a gift of self to the other and to spend time, heart, and soul serving the other. Love is thinking of the good of the other and showing this thoughtfulness in words and deeds.

• *The gift of self to the other, communion of persons, physical intimacy, and the act of breastfeeding are all connected with the concepts in the Pope's theology of the body.* It is through her body that a mother gives milk, love, and comfort to her baby and forms a deep communion with and commitment to him. Father Virtue writes that "the gift of nursing her infant is a maternal sign of the donative meaning of the body in the Communion of Persons."[82]

• *Both acts involve a love that unifies two persons, according to the definition of* love *given by Pope John Paul II in his book* Love and Responsibility.[83] I believe that this unifying love can be experienced by both husband and wife and also by the breastfeeding mother and her baby. In fact, "The greater the feeling of responsibility for the person, the more true love there is."[84] Certainly there is a grave responsibility to give an infant the very best of care when a mother chooses to breastfeed.

The Pope in his earlier days said that love never *utilizes* a person. This is especially true with breastfeeding. A mother learns to give to her baby by the very fact that she is breastfeeding. She is constantly giving to her baby. Her reward comes when her baby learns to love her in return and soon becomes a very affectionate child. The baby soon has eyes only for his mother and will usually kick happily or show bodily signs of happiness when his mother gets ready to nurse him. It is very difficult for a mother to abuse her baby or to use her baby for other purposes. On the other hand, abuses in the marriage relationship are observed frequently in our society.

• *Both acts have two orders: the order of nature and the personal order.* In *Love and Responsibility,* Pope John Paul II also speaks frequently of the marriage relationship. His discourse on the sexual relationship between husband and wife may also apply to the breastfeeding relationship between mother and child. The Pope discusses two orders involved in the sexual relationship: the natural order and the personal order. These two orders, he says, cannot be separated because "each depends upon the other."[85]

The Pope says that the natural order in the sexual relationship has reproduction as its object. The same can be said about breastfeeding, which also has as its object the completion of the reproductive cycle. Remember that the reproductive cycle ends with breastfeeding, not after childbirth, because the baby's total dependence upon the mother's body for protection and nutrition occurs both during pregnancy and during the early months of breastfeeding. In addition, reproduction depends upon the fertility-infertility cycle of the woman. The infertility of the woman during pregnancy continues during breastfeeding for months or a year or two.

The personal order of the sexual relationship between husband and wife has love as its object, and this love is expressed between the two persons involved. The same personal order also applies to breastfeeding. The personal order of the breastfeeding relationship between mother and baby has love as its object, and this love is expressed between the two persons involved.

Thus, the two orders — the natural order and the personal order — of the sexual relationship between man and woman are also present in the breastfeeding relationship between mother and baby. In God's plan, both relationships have a natural order and a personal order that depend on each other; the objects of each order, for the marriage act and for the breastfeeding act, are reproduction and self-giving love.

Chapter Six

∞

Natural Child Spacing

There are two basic forms of Natural Family Planning (NFP) for natural conception regulation: systematic Natural Family Planning and ecological breastfeeding. Systematic NFP refers to a system of observing, recording, and interpreting the woman's signs of fertility. With this informed awareness of the fertile and infertile times of the female cycle, couples seeking to avoid a pregnancy abstain from the marriage act during the fertile time. Conversely, those couples desiring a child seek pregnancy during the most fertile days of the cycle.

Ecological breastfeeding is the second form of natural conception regulation. This form of breastfeeding generally postpones the return of fertility for many months after childbirth. You probably have heard that the saying "breastfeeding spaces babies" is an old wives' tale. In a way, this statement is true, because the sort of limited breastfeeding that is common in Western culture generally has a very limited baby-spacing effect. On the other hand, ecological breastfeeding, which I will describe, generally postpones the return of fertility for over a year and does space babies.

My interest and enjoyment in nursing my babies came before my interest in natural child spacing. I am aware, however, that many women will become interested in natural child spacing first and grow to enjoy the breastfeeding relationship later, gradually coming to appreciate the other benefits of breastfeeding. The use of breastfeeding to space the births of children is one way to follow the Church's exhortation to be generous in having children and its admonition to avoid the use of any contraceptive drugs, devices, or behaviors. Many couples, in forming their families, have used breastfeeding alone for many years while having their children.

∽

Mothering practices do make a difference

My understanding of natural child spacing came about very gradually. Pregnant with our first baby, I attended monthly meetings of La Leche League, an organization that offers information about and support for breastfeeding throughout the United States. After the birth of our first baby, I continued to attend these meetings, where I heard about natural child spacing, so I asked my Catholic obstetrician about it. He told me that no matter how I nursed my baby, I would have a period within three months after childbirth. This statement is false, but in this case, my doctor was right about my first period. It returned within three months after childbirth.

With my second baby, I also nursed frequently day and night. I was seeing at that time a different Catholic obstetrician who was a promoter of the "temperature method" of NFP. This doctor knew I wanted to breastfeed, so instead of recommending the temperature method, he advised me to breastfeed my baby exclusively. He made it clear that I was not to offer my baby any other liquids or solids. He asked that I call him as soon as I had my first period.

Regarding mothering practices, I changed greatly in our second baby's early days. For various reasons, I began sleeping with my baby for a nap and during the night, and I quit using a pacifier, to which my daughter had developed a skin allergy. We began to change our views on babysitters; they were no longer desirable for our nursing babies. I believe God was preparing or guiding my husband and me to follow more closely his plan for babies, mostly because of my interest in his plan for spacing babies.

With my second baby, my period returned at twelve months postpartum, but I forgot to call my doctor. Now I regret not calling him. I wish I had thanked him for that advice! By the time our baby was a year old, we were busy getting ready to move to Canada. We were also thinking about having another baby.

The long absence of menstruation with our second baby was due to the changes in my mothering style. However, I was not to realize fully this until later.

∽

The return of fertility varied

Menstruation returned soon after childbirth with one baby and at twelve months with the other baby. Why the difference between these two experiences? After all, I had learned at the La Leche League meetings that frequent nursing was important in order to keep up an adequate milk supply. With both babies, I nursed frequently day and night.

I began doing research to find an answer. Why did some people claim that breastfeeding spaced babies? Why did others say it didn't work? A close friend of mine encouraged me to write a book about it. I spent many hours going over research at my alma mater, the University of California at San Francisco, and later at the Public Health library near our home in Canada. My search resulted in two published studies and my book *Breastfeeding and Natural Child Spacing*.

If you would like breastfeeding to space your babies, I strongly encourage you to read *Breastfeeding and Natural Child Spacing*. It's the only book on the subject, and our society does not generally support or encourage the type of breastfeeding associated with extended natural infertility. You may experience unfriendly comments about your style of mothering from parents, relatives, friends, and the medical profession. *Breastfeeding and Natural Child Spacing* will offer you encouragement and give you the know-how and support you need to practice and enjoy the natural mothering lifestyle even though you live in a typical Western culture.

∽

On the trail of breastfeeding infertility research

During those early years of research in the Sixties, I found ample studies showing that breastfeeding could impact the reproductive system and keep the ovaries at rest. Those published studies dated from the Thirties through the Sixties. The conclusions of these earlier studies are quite similar to the conclusions of recent studies.[86] As with today's studies, the earlier studies stressed the importance of the baby's suckling to inhibit ovulation and concluded that early supplementation caused an early return of fertility. A few prior studies hinted at the importance of *exclusive* breastfeeding, which was then called complete or total breastfeeding.

As I studied the research and looked into my own mothering practices, I began to realize that there was more to breastfeeding infertility than exclusive breastfeeding. Many mothers who exclusively breastfed experienced an early return of menstruation. This became clear to me at my first La Leche League meetings and in my later work as a La Leche League leader. There had to be other factors involved.

Then I found the answer. The key to natural breastfeeding infertility revolved around a *form of mothering* that allowed for two important practices: frequent nursing and unrestricted nursing. Frequent nursing refers to regular periodic nursing day and night.

Unrestricted nursing means that the baby is allowed to nurse for a long period at the breast. This usually happens when the baby nurses into a deep sleep or when he is lying next to his mother, such as during the night or during his mother's nap. Sometimes unrestricted nursing occurs when the baby needs security; for example, he hurts himself or is in a new environment.

It became clear to me that mothering practices *do* directly affect the amount of nursing that occurs at the breast. The breast is a wonderful mothering tool. When the mother provides all of her baby's nourishment, plus the greater part of his other suckling needs, at her breast during the early months, the mother will almost invariably experience the side effect of natural infertility.

∞

The norm of breastfeeding amenorrhea

The spacing of human births is the plan of the Author of Life. Why? Because caring for a baby in a natural way, by breastfeeding, results in breastfeeding amenorrhea, or the absence of menstruation during breastfeeding. With extended breastfeeding, amenorrhea occurs over an extended period — one to two years or longer.

This norm of extended amenorrhea is so unusual in North America and most European cultures that I would like to repeat clearly: for a *nursing* mother to go one year, two years, three years, or even longer without any menstrual cycles is *normal*, even if not average.

Occasionally a doctor seeing a nursing mother will look at her amenorrhea as a sickness. One physician wouldn't give a mother credit for a normal checkup, which would have been covered by insurance, because of her lengthy breastfeeding amenorrhea. (She fought it and won.) Another nursing mother was told by her otherwise great physician that she should wean her baby to see whether her periods would come back or if something was wrong with her! But remember, a nursing mother in amenorrhea is usually a very healthy person. She is only experiencing one of the healthy benefits of breastfeeding: natural infertility or natural child spacing.

∞

Ecological breastfeeding

The only type of breastfeeding that is associated with extended natural infertility is "ecological breastfeeding." This is a term I coined to distinguish the type of breastfeeding that normally delays the return of fertility for a significant time from those types of breastfeeding that usually *do not* delay the return of fertility. Ecological breastfeeding almost always provides the frequent and unrestricted nursing that is required for natural infertility. With ecological breastfeeding, the mother uses her own breasts to nourish and nurture her infant. She does not use pacifiers or bottles. Her breasts provide the comfort nursing and extra suckling that so many babies need. The main characteristic of ecological breastfeeding is mother-baby togetherness. If the mother remains with her baby, she will find ecological breastfeeding relatively easy to follow.

∞

The Seven Standards of ecological breastfeeding

There are seven characteristics or requirements of ecological breastfeeding. These characteristics were the basis for my research in earlier years. I now call them the Seven Standards to make it clear they are the norm, not just vague guidelines or suggestions. They are the rules to follow if you desire natural spacing of children through breastfeeding:

1. Exclusively breastfeed for the first six months of life.

2. Pacify your baby at your breasts.[87]

3. Don't use bottles and pacifiers. This includes not using pumps.[88]

4. Sleep with your baby for night feedings.[89]

5. Sleep with your baby for a daily-nap feeding.[90]

6. Nurse frequently day and night, and avoid strict schedules.

7. Avoid any practice that restricts nursing or separates you from your baby.

Each of the Seven Standards is important; each helps to ensure that frequent and unrestricted nursing will occur. Together they almost invariably delay the return of fertility.

I often tell people that the Seven Standards can be looked at as a pie, an "ecological" pie or an "infertility" pie, with seven pieces. You need all seven pieces to be complete. Following only two or three standards generally does not provide much delay in the return of fertility.

∞

At six months, only six standards

Sometime between six and eight months of age, the baby usually begins to take other foods. Thus, the "exclusive breastfeeding rule" or Standard 1, no longer applies. Only Standards 2 through 7 are now in use. At this time, the baby continues to nurse frequently, and the amount of nursing usually decreases very gradually. If the baby gets sick, he may increase his nursing at the breast. The mother's amenorrhea usually continues for a long time if the breastfeeding continues to be frequent and unrestricted.

Breastfeeding and Catholic Motherhood

Our society tells us not to nurse frequently, but frequent nursing is the norm for ecological breastfeeding. If you are down to only six or seven feedings throughout a twenty-four-hour day, you can expect fertility to return soon — if it hasn't already.

∞

Duration of natural infertility

The duration of breastfeeding's natural infertility depends on the type of nursing.

First eight weeks: According to a consensus of breastfeeding experts, the mother who is doing *exclusive* breastfeeding is infertile during the *first eight weeks postpartum (or first fifty-six days postpartum)* even if she has vaginal bleeding during that time.[91] This information is very helpful, has been tested by research, and applies also to the *ecologically* breastfeeding mother who is doing exclusive breastfeeding during this time.

First three months: During the first three months postpartum, ecological breastfeeding naturally suppresses the return of fertility almost all the time. That is, during the first three months after childbirth, the chance of pregnancy is practically nil *if:*

• The mother is ecologically breastfeeding (following the Seven Standards).

• The mother has no menstrual bleeding after the eighth week or after the fifty-sixth day.[92]

First six months: During the next three months, the chance of pregnancy is 1 percent *if:*

• The mother is ecologically or exclusively breastfeeding.

• The mother has no menstruation.[93]

Thus, ecological breastfeeding can provide a 99-percent natural infertility rate during the first six months postpartum, provided the mother has not had a menstruation. Ninety-three percent of ecologically breastfeeding mothers will be in amenorrhea at six months postpartum, about 56 percent will remain in amenorrhea at twelve months postpartum, and about one-third will still be in amenorrhea at eighteen months postpartum.[94] Many couples discover that breastfeeding alone provides eighteen to thirty months of spacing between the births of their children.

If a couple has an early return of fertility while breastfeeding and they require further spacing of children, they can switch to systemic NFP and continue the nursing as long as they desire. A couple can successfully practice systematic NFP while the wife is breastfeeding. The NFP charts of a nursing mother who has resumed fertile cycles are very similar to the NFP charts of a non-nursing mother with fertile cycles.

In a few cases, fertility returns during amenorrhea for the nursing mother, but this can be observed with fertility awareness. If the amenorrhea is unusually long, the couple may also choose to use systematic NFP or fertility awareness in an effort to achieve pregnancy when fertility finally returns. When menstruation returns, sometimes it takes a few cycles before pregnancy can be achieved. NFP is explained in much greater depth in *The Art of Natural Family Planning*,[95] the manual I co-authored with my husband, John.

∽

Natural child spacing
and Church teaching

As mothers, we choose breastfeeding first and foremost because it is best for our babies. When you follow this natural plan for feeding babies, you soon discover the many side benefits, one being the extended natural infertility. The teachings of the Catholic Church fully support using breastfeeding with the hope of a natural spacing of babies.

When I pick up a Catholic book on marriage and family or on NFP, I always check the index for the word *breastfeeding*. I'm usually disappointed, because breastfeeding is usually absent from these books. I was recently elated, however, to find a book that covered this topic quite well. In his book, *The Splendor of Love: John Paul II's Vision for Marriage and Family*,[96] Father Walter Schu wrote that ecological breastfeeding was "an integral part of Natural Family Planning" and "a natural way God has provided to space babies about two years apart." Father Schu offers an excellent summary of ecological breastfeeding, emphasizes the need for frequent nursing for spacing the births of children, and lists some benefits of breastfeeding.

The *Catechism of the Catholic Church* states: "For just reason, spouses may wish to space the births of their children." The *Catechism* reminds couples to be generous in having children and to not be guided by selfish reasons (n. 2368). Many couples using breastfeeding alone to space babies are open to having children as they come. However, for those couples using systematic NFP or breastfeeding, the reminder to remain generous to life is always good to hear.

In *Humanae Vitae*, the following passages definitely pertain to breastfeeding:

• God has wisely arranged the natural laws and times of fertility so that successive births are naturally spaced (n 11).

• The teaching of the Church about the proper spacing of children is a promulgation of the divine law itself (n 22).

Thus, another one of the many gifts that God has given us through breastfeeding is the ability to follow the teachings of his Church; allowing us to space the births of our children safely, naturally, and morally!

∽

Chapter Seven

Early Parenting Goals

When you are expecting a baby — especially your first — there are some simple parenting goals to begin considering. These goals deal with choices involving breastfeeding and the first three years of life.

∽

Adapt to circumstances

One thing you may have absorbed from this book is the ordinary obligation for new parents to try to breastfeed their children. I sympathize with the many women who have wanted to nurse their baby but couldn't or who had great difficulty doing so. But if a mother is unable to breastfeed, she can mimic nature in several ways. She can still take her child with her wherever she goes; she can nap with her baby; she can be the only one to feed the baby, and she can feed the baby in the nursing position when she offers her baby the bottle. In this way, she can provide many of the nurturing benefits of breastfeeding.

Women who *have* to work can still breastfeed. Almost every breastfeeding organization, breastfeeding book, or breastfeeding conference has ample information for the working breastfeeding mother. She will most likely not be able to do ecological breastfeeding and experience extended amenorrhea. She will, however, be able to give her baby many of the benefits of breastfeeding.

Breastfeeding and Catholic Motherhood

We often hear of women who are unable to breastfeed. Fortunately, that is rarely the case with proper education. With support and accurate information, almost all women can breastfeed. Many experts say that almost all women are physically able to breastfeed their babies.

In a bottle-feeding culture, breastfeeding mothers need support. A husband's strong support of breastfeeding is most valuable to his wife and will help her to continue in this task. Breastfeeding usually goes well immediately after childbirth. If obstacles occur, they usually subside, and eventually the breastfeeding goes smoothly.

To avoid breastfeeding problems and to learn how to cope with those that might arise, you can attend breastfeeding meetings during pregnancy. These meetings should be conducted by women who have successfully nursed their babies. New mothers should form friendships with mothers who have been successful at breastfeeding. Sometimes these friendships begin at breastfeeding meetings or in your church setting and last a lifetime.

Another idea is to form a nursing mothers' group in your parish, perhaps headed by a volunteer lactation consultant, or an active or retired La Leche League leader, or a stay-at-home female doctor. You could ask local breastfeeding experts to speak at your group. A local priest, deacon, or nun who is enthusiastic about breastfeeding might be willing to visit your group once a year and give a talk to encourage mothers. Your group could offer tips on how to be successful at breastfeeding during the important early weeks and months of breastfeeding. You could study the lives of married female saints or the saints canonized by John Paul II. Or you could simply meet for a play date once a week and offer each other support about breastfeeding. When a mother has a new baby, each member of your group could make a meal for her. You could also give a new mother or an expectant mother a book about breastfeeding. And don't forget to invite to your group the rare mother who is not able to breastfeed — for whatever reason. The most important job of a mother is to love and guide her children, whether she can breastfeed or not.

When a mother has difficulty breastfeeding, I recommend that she pray to the Blessed Mother. This has helped many women I have known, including one of my daughters. Overall, breastfeeding is an occasion to grow closer to God; a quiet time when we can pray, reflect, and ask for help from above.

If you have help after childbirth, you should make sure that the helpers are enthusiastic about breastfeeding. If anyone recommends weaning as the solution to a problem, first check out this advice with breastfeeding experts. Usually weaning is not necessary, or cessation of nursing need be only temporary. Up-to-date information is available in the La Leche League manual, *The Womanly Art of Breastfeeding*.[97] A mother with a breastfeeding problem may seek counseling from a local La Leche League leader. You can find a La Leche League leader in your state at their website: www.lalecheleague.org.

Today breastfeeding advice or counseling has become much more advanced, and thus, more women are being helped. For example, in 2003, two friends of mine suffered extreme pain while breastfeeding their newborns. Both of their babies had tongue-tie or a tight frenulum. The frenulum was taken care of (without anesthesia) and the breastfeeding continued after the procedure without pain.[98] Having the right resources and professionals, these two mothers were able to continue breastfeeding and finally to enjoy nursing their babies. Without this support, they would have weaned their babies. It needs repeating that almost all women can breastfeed if they have a healthy baby and the proper information and support.

∽

*Exclusively breastfeed your
baby for the first six months*

No matter what your other parenting or family-planning ob-
jectives, the first goal is to nurse exclusively for the first six months
of life. This means offering only your milk as food for your baby,
directly from your breasts if at all possible. There is no need to offer bottles, pacifiers, early liquids, early solids, or water. As we
have seen, exclusive breastfeeding for the first six months of life is
recommended by the American Academy of Pediatrics and the
American Academy of Family Physicians. It is strongly endorsed
by the World Health Organization, UNICEF, and experts who
promote breastfeeding.

For many possible reasons, of course, some mothers will not be
able to nurse exclusively for six months. In these cases, four
months of exclusive breastfeeding is better than two months of exclusive breastfeeding, and two months of exclusive breastfeeding
is better than none at all! While the preferred health goal is six
months of exclusive breastfeeding, anything short of that goal or
any amount of nursing is better than none at all.

Here's why. Those babies who are exclusively breastfed for
three months are far healthier during the first year of life compared with those babies who are never breastfed.

According to a 1999 study, during the first year of life, one
thousand babies who were never breastfed had 2,033 more office
visits, 212 more days of hospitalization, and 609 more prescrip-
tions for only three illnesses (lower-respiratory-tract illnesses,
otitis media [ear infection], and gastrointestinal illnesses) compared with another thousand babies who were exclusively breast-
fed for only three months. "The excess total direct medical costs
incurred by never-breast-fed infants during the first year of life for

these three illnesses alone was between $331 and $475 *more than* the costs incurred by breast-fed infants."[99]

Another study reviewed common illnesses among babies, such as diarrhea, coughs and wheezing, vomiting, pneumonia, ear infections, runny nose, and fever. There were two conclusions from this study. First, every baby benefits from the protective effect of exclusive breastfeeding, even when clean water, good sanitation, and hygienic infant formula are available. Second, the protective effect of breastfeeding for these common illnesses was noticed only with exclusive breastfeeding — not with minimal breastfeeding.[100]

Any goal of exclusive breastfeeding up to six months or of almost-exclusive breastfeeding is an excellent choice in caring for your baby.

∾

Breastfeed for at least one year

The American Academy of Family Physicians and the American Academy of Pediatrics encourage American mothers to nurse for at least one year. This is a reasonable goal even for working mothers.

Many mothers who enjoy breastfeeding may decide to continue to nurse their baby longer than one year. Some mothers imagine nursing a one-year-old unappealing until they find themselves in that relationship and then decide to continue. They enjoy nursing, they see that the baby enjoys it, so they see no reason to wean.

Interestingly, the AAFP, in its position paper on breastfeeding, although setting the goal of nursing for one year, also discourages weaning during the first two years of life because "the child [under two years of age] is at increased risk of illness if weaned."[101] Mothers who decide to nurse their babies beyond the first birthday can find support for their decision from two organizations that encourage mothers to nurse for at least two years: UNICEF and the WHO. Likewise, Pope John Paul II supports this two-year recommendation.

Through breastfeeding, the baby receives immunity from his mother. The immediate protective effect of breast milk has been well stated by Dr. Jack Newman:

> If a mother is exposed to cholera bacteria, within hours of that exposure, her milk will contain SIgA [an antibody] specifically made against cholera bacteria. The baby is continually protected against those particular bacteria in his immediate environment, or at least the immediate environment of his mother, which is usually the same thing. Or if she is exposed to influenza virus, within hours of her being exposed, her milk will contain antibodies specifically directed against influenza virus. This is miraculous. Formula will never be able to replicate this — never.[102]

Nursing your baby for one year is an excellent choice in giving your baby the best start in life. If you achieve or almost achieve that goal, you are to be commended.

∞

Remain with your child during the early years

One additional parenting goal — whether you breastfeed or not — is to remain with your child during the early years, if at all possible. Wise teachers, parents, and Church leaders have echoed this message for years. Yet today it is often muffled by the louder voices advocating financial success and materialism.

These voices usually urge mothers to put their child in day care. Last year, one of my daughters, after hearing that advice over and over, told me, "If I hear one more person say anything about day care, I will scream!" A mother usually won't get encouragement to stay home with her children from those professionals or media reporters who have chosen to have their own children raised by others for a good part of the day. They see nothing wrong with recommending substitute care for others. Parents should likewise beware of doctors who give excellent medical advice but offer parenting suggestions that contradict their own choices.

Certain decisions made prior to the arrival of children may make it difficult to be a full-time mother and to nurse your children. For one example, debts can make it difficult for a mother to stay home, so going back to work is often given as a reason for weaning. Thus, your family's financial health can impact breast-feeding and subsequently the health, happiness, and development of your baby.

Many pre-marital (and/or pre-child) decisions, such as not owning an expensive car, living at home, and attending a local college or university, help a person to eliminate or minimize debts. Wrong decisions prior to marriage may later force a woman to remain in the workplace once children arrive.

Parents might encourage careers for their daughters that make mothering at home possible if their daughters are called to marriage and motherhood. Men who want their wives to remain home with their children need to make decisions that allow them to enter marriage without an excessive debt on their shoulders. With proper choices prior to and after the wedding, the goal of the mother staying home with her children is within reach.

Mothers who are dedicated to taking care of their own children make many sacrifices for their children and often lack support in our society and even from the Church. Certain popes, however, as you have seen in chapter 3, have offered stay-at-home mothers their moral support. They value the role of motherhood and the work that goes into raising children.[103]

∞

Your care is the best care

I have written about the irreplaceable role of the mother, the right for the baby to be cared for by his mother, the importance of breast milk for the health of the baby, and the need for the baby to have that one consistent caregiver as shown by research. The best care, the care that God intends for all babies in today's world, is to have that needed single consistent caregiver and to receive milk from his mother, especially during the early years.

Let us recall Pope John Paul II's remarks about mothering and breastfeeding from 1995: "So vital is this interaction between mother and child. . . . No one can substitute for the mother in this natural activity."

Chapter Eight

∽

Perseverance

When you first begin to breastfeed your baby, you may encounter situations you didn't anticipate. You may experience difficulty with breastfeeding. You may feel uncomfortable when nursing in public or unfamiliar places, and you may experience negative comments, especially as your baby grows older. You may sense that people expect you to attend social events but leave your baby at home.

You may also find your life changing in other ways. Your parenting style may need to adapt. You may need to adjust your expectations, schedules, and habits — when it comes to prayer, for example.

I'd like to share my encounters with some of these difficulties and help you learn to practice the most important breastfeeding virtue: perseverance.

∽

Breastfeeding difficulties

When I started breastfeeding as a young mother, I encountered the usual minor problems: engorgement, tender spots in the breast area, and sore nipples. Fortunately, these problems can be easily solved with time and proper care. With engorgement, you can learn to express the excess milk manually until your breast feels comfortable again. If you have a tender or painful area in the breast, you can usually relieve it by having your baby do lots of nursing on the affected breast. Sleeping with your baby during a nap allows your baby to suckle a lot on the affected breast, giving you extra rest and alleviating the situation. This also generally helps avoid more serious situations, such as mastitis.

With our fourth baby, I experienced a severe case of nipple soreness. The creams recommended for treatment did not work. The situation was so bad, it hurt to have a nightgown or shirt touch my breast. After trying everything, I called an older friend. She said the only thing that gave her relief was the warm air from a portable hair dryer! I plugged in my hair dryer near my bed and applied the warm air repeatedly when I had a minute or two. I made sure I applied the warm air after a nursing to dry off the nipples. I found this simple remedy gave me relief almost immediately and was an answer to my prayers. Soon I no longer needed the hair dryer.

Sometimes a breast-fed baby can develop nursing habits that irritate or hurt you. The baby may use his hand to play with the other nipple, with a mole, or with your skin while nursing. A simple no, or holding the baby's hand, usually is effective in stopping the undesirable behavior.

Some babies bite. This may cause you, without thinking, to cry out painfully and upset your baby. Try inserting your finger into the baby's mouth to release his hold on the nipple. The baby thus learns from his mother's reaction that his mother is unhappy. When he goes back to the breast and nurses properly, you can express your pleasure to the baby and maybe even sing softly to him. Your sweet behavior lets the baby know that his nursing is now acceptable. The same goes for a baby who is constantly doing gymnastics while nursing!

Occasionally a baby insists on nursing only when the mother is in a certain position: sitting up or lying down. Likewise, with firmness and kindness you can train your baby to understand that breastfeeding is to be done in more than one position.

When you have a breastfeeding problem, prayer helps. Through prayer God often leads you to the right source or person for help. One lady I counseled thanked me for my prayer advice and told me how much it helped her to pray for Mary's help during her times of nursing difficulty.

It is important not to give up. Pray and persevere. Contact those in your community who might have the right information. Call a friend who has had a lot of breastfeeding experience. Search breastfeeding websites. One helpful resource is our own website: www.NaturalFamilyPlanningAndMore.org.[104]

∞

Nursing in front of others

Horrors! This was my first reaction as a new breastfeeding mother. I was scared to death to nurse in front of other people. I attended La Leche League meetings during and after my first pregnancy because our childbirth instructor highly recommended them, and I gained a lot of helpful information on breastfeeding and family nutrition. But on those occasions when I had to nurse my baby during a meeting, I went into "hiding." I left the meetings temporarily and would find a quiet room where I could nurse in private.

Gradually, experience changed all that. Looking back, I remember when John and I went to visit a friend named Bernadette. During the visit, our baby wanted to nurse, so I asked Bernadette if I could go into her bedroom to nurse. She couldn't understand why I would want to retire to her bedroom when all I wanted to do was something so natural as nursing my baby! She was so understanding of my situation that I felt very comfortable nursing in her presence. That was the beginning of my adventure of gradually learning to nurse in different situations outside our home.

I learned to nurse modestly at church, on hiking trails, in restaurants, at meetings, and in many other situations. Most people around me weren't even aware that I was nursing. I went from leaving my nursing baby at home when I had to run errands to taking the baby with me everywhere. In church I used a summer shawl during the hot months and a longer wool shawl during the cold months; these provided a "cove" of privacy. I would sit at the end of a pew with my husband on the other side of me, or I would sit between family members. In a restaurant, I would try to sit at a side table, not one in the center of the room. I learned to wear bras and clothing that made the breast accessible in a modest way.

I'm still amazed at the ingenuity of some mothers when it comes to modest breastfeeding. By modest nursing, I mean no part of the breast is exposed. One husband I know would hold up a blanket in front of his wife when she nursed in church or in front of others. Another time I saw a woman in church wear a large beautiful red scarf that was tied around her neck and covered her shoulders. The point of the folded scarf fell down the center of her back. When her baby wanted to nurse, she swung the scarf around to conceal what was going on. Even with all my years of nursing, I found her approach fascinating.

It doesn't matter how modest nursing is achieved. What counts is that you feel confident and comfortable when nursing among acquaintances or strangers.

You will gain confidence as you gain experience. One mom I know asked her pastor if he would provide a chair for her in the women's restroom so she could nurse her baby. He was happy to oblige her. But soon she found she didn't need the chair. She soon gained enough confidence to nurse in the pew.

Another lady found her comfort in a saint. I'd like to share her experience, as she related it to me, since many of us have had these feelings when confronted with nursing for the first time in public:

When I started nursing, I remember how shy, timid, and self-conscious I felt about it. I recall being at a moms-and-tots playgroup at church and being mortified when my thirteen- or fourteen-month-old wanted to nurse! After all, she had had her first birthday! After that incident, I turned to Blessed Father Solanus Casey in prayer, holding in my hand a relic a friend had given us. In my heart, I was agonizing about what to do if my little child wanted to nurse in public. Should I wean her because that seemed more socially acceptable? But I didn't really want to. When I said a little prayer, asking his help, in my mind's eye Blessed Solanus Casey and I were talking, sitting across the desk from each other. In a kindly, paternal way, he patted my hand and said, "You're the mother; you know what is best for your child." And immediately I felt peace and an immense relief and clear direction. That makes it easy. As a mother, I wanted to nurse my little child when he needed to! Now I don't give it a second thought as I discreetly nurse our twenty-two-month-old at church or anywhere!

There will always be a few people who will never accept "public" nursing — even modest public nursing. By public nursing I mean nursing in situations where people other than your husband and children or a close relative are present. Nursing in your home with guests present would be considered public nursing in this sense.

Eventually, most mothers do become comfortable with modest public nursing. Mothers and babies belong together, and mothers are true role models, real winners, when they do what is best for their baby.

∾

Negative attitudes from others

I was once told by a public-health nurse that I couldn't breast-feed a nine-month-old because my milk would be sour! That ridiculous comment would always draw a laugh when I shared it with other nursing moms, but it could have had a negative impact upon a new mother who didn't know better.

Sometimes you will experience negative comments even from people ordinarily sympathetic to your breastfeeding and parenting goals. I became a La Leche League leader in Canada and had a strong influence among the new mothers, who were quite open to nursing for one or two years. A move to Salina, Kansas, brought me into a group where early weaning was common. My co-leader weaned when her baby was eight months old, but was very open to the fact that I was still nursing a child eighteen months old. However, I began to feel my child was not welcome at the meetings. One mother in the group debated me at a meeting and argued there was no benefit to nursing a child past nine months. In those days — the late Sixties — the ample research we have today, supporting breastfeeding for at least one year, was largely nonexistent.

In our society, people often compliment a mother for breastfeeding her small baby. But attitudes can change as your baby nears his first birthday. Sometimes a critical or sarcastic comment will hurt your feelings and perhaps make you doubt yourself. It is at these times that support from your husband and others can be especially helpful. Whenever I see a mother nursing her baby modestly anywhere, I always try to say something to compliment her — even if she's a complete stranger.

While the nursing mother is learning how to deal with breast-feeding, the husband needs to learn about its merits. A husband is generally more receptive to breastfeeding, even breastfeeding an older baby, if he reads material on the subject or attends a breast-feeding conference with his wife. At breastfeeding conferences, there are usually one or two workshops available for dads only. I encourage couples to try to develop friendships with other Catholic couples who feel strongly about breastfeeding. These friend-ships give you support in your parenting choices as well as support in the Faith.

When I was breastfeeding, I had very little support from fellow Catholics once we moved from California. I remember spending an evening at the home of Catholic friends and feeling saddened to find out that the host couple had taken their baby and other young child over to Grandma's. We were the only couple there with our baby. I remember thinking at the time that our friends were probably wondering why we brought her in the first place, because she slept the entire time! Years later, we moved to Cin-cinnati, where I nursed two babies without much support. Even-tually I did find breastfeeding support among fellow Catholics, but I no longer needed it then. I wish we had had this support during our earlier years of parenting. It would have made breastfeeding so much easier. I hope you, too, can find breastfeeding support in your circle of friends, especially Catholic friends.

∞

Avoiding separations

Oftentimes, the first question a new nursing mother asks is: "What do I do when I want to go somewhere?" Mothers who ask that question assume the answer is to leave the baby at home. But experienced breastfeeding moms will often reply by telling of the emotional trauma that prolonged separation can cause in both mother and baby.

Child-care experts sometimes do a disservice to nursing mothers when they promote the use of a bottle once a day so that the mother does not have to feel "tied to the house." Oftentimes that mother will begin to use the bottle more and more, until she is no longer nursing. Even a mother who nurses quite frequently and offers a bottle once a day usually finds such a practice fruitless as the baby ages and wants only Mom.

If you surround yourself with successful nursing mothers, you will hear them tell you that it is usually easier to take your baby with you. I found the *togetherness* lifestyle with my baby much more enjoyable and workable than the *separation* lifestyle I once had with my first baby (even though we still did many things together).

My husband also changed tremendously. With our first baby, he believed it was beneficial for the baby to have the experience of many babysitters. Eventually he came to believe that mother is best and that having a lot of different caretakers was actually harmful to a baby.

Being different is not easy. I was the oddball when I went to a Catholic school parents' meeting and was the only one there who brought her baby. I was the oddball when I attended a college faculty party with our baby on my back. I was the oddball when I volunteered to teach dental health to several kindergarten classes and brought my baby and another small child with me. I was the oddball when I taught mothering classes at a Catholic school to seventh- and eighth-grade girls and brought my three-year-old with me. I took my baby or small children with me whenever I gave a talk at breastfeeding conferences. Of course, there were times when my husband was home and cared for the older children. But he was often traveling, too, and I had no choice but to take the children with me.

When you are with your child all the time, you know how he will behave away from home. I appeared on television once with my nursing toddler because she was content to sit at my feet and play with toys. She was not a wandering child. If I had a toddler who liked to take off, I would have had to make other arrangements! In fact, I did have such a child and made arrangements for her older sister to come along to watch this wandering child whenever I promoted breastfeeding. When we taught NFP classes in the evenings, this nursing baby/toddler came with us, but our older daughters took turns caring for him at the classes.

Take your baby with you to church. Quiet happy noises from a baby usually do not cause a disturbance. And although loud noises, loud talking, or crying can disturb those in prayer, in such situations you can take the child to the back or to an enclosed children's area. Etiquette requires the consideration of others at any social event or church service; it shouldn't require you to leave your baby home.

There will be times when you cannot do something because you are breastfeeding. Twice I passed up opportunities to go to Rome with my husband (and a chance to meet the Pope!) because I was needed at home. I know one couple who were awarded a wonderful cruise trip from the husband's employer, but they turned it down because their nursing baby couldn't go.

There will be times when you will have to make sacrifices so that your breastfeeding relationship with your baby can continue uninterrupted. But the confidence you gain from the breastfeeding experience — and the strong belief that you're doing the right thing for your child — should enable you to bear such sacrifices, even joyfully.

Breastfeeding and Catholic Motherhood

∽

Finding time for prayer and holiness

A few nursing mothers I know have felt guilty that they didn't have the time to do more for their spiritual life. They apparently saw the strength of their spiritual lives tied directly to the number of daily Masses they attended or the number of holy hours they kept. They could not see their spiritual life growing within the walls of their own home. But as a mother of young children, this is primarily where you will find your holiness deepening — at home.

As married women, we chose motherhood, not the religious life. Our Lord does not ask us to live in a monastery. We seek holiness within our families. The first step to such holiness is to try to do well what we are supposed to do as spouses and as parents, even if that sometimes means missing a weekday Mass, a Bible study, or a holy hour.

Please don't get me wrong. I think daily Mass and weekly holy hours are wonderful practices, but each family is different. Each family is thus different in its response to God. Maybe one family is called to attend daily Mass. Maybe another is called to attend Mass only one extra weekday or to pray the Rosary instead of going to daily Mass. Some families may feel lucky to get in one decade of the family Rosary each day, while another family aims for one Rosary a week. Some mothers homeschool several children and are consumed with that responsibility. Some families feel overwhelmed caring for an elderly parent or for a child who has special problems or needs.

I know some Catholic mothers who have felt like losers after they attended a Catholic conference where speakers strongly recommended daily Mass, or even urged it as a necessity for raising a good Catholic family. There are certainly reasons young Catholic families do not or cannot get to daily Mass. Certainly the mothers of these families are not losers, but can be real winners in the spiritual life if they attend to the primary needs of their vocation. Maybe your "holy hour" for the week is spent helping someone else or taking care of an important matter in the home. Your child needs an extra lesson in math, or your stressed-out husband needs your attention.

Some busy mothers manage to find some time to grow spiritually. Some try to get up fifteen minutes early to read Scripture and spend some time with the Lord. You may find time to say a Rosary when you put the baby in the stroller for a quick walk. If you have a dog, you can put your baby on your back, take the dog for a walk, and pray your Rosary all at the same time. Grace before meals is another way to be thankful to God for food, family, and friends, and for his many other blessings. Nursing can be another time to contemplate God's goodness and to be thankful for the baby in your arms.

Some mothers use the nursing time itself as an opportunity for prayer. Looking back over my many years of nursing, I don't remember using nursing as prayer time. I also rarely used it to watch TV or to read a book. I used the time to enjoy my baby and deepen my bond with him.

On the other hand, I did find breastfeeding to be a time of reflection about God's goodness. There are certain times or places where I stand in awe of God's beauty and marvelous works. Standing by the ocean always lifts my mind to God. Hiking to the top of a mountain and overlooking a beautiful valley has the same effect. And seeing the miracle of life in my baby always made me grateful for God's gift to my husband and me. This sense of gratitude to God can be a moment of true prayer for you when you breastfeed your baby in the quiet of your home.

Of course, as your children grow and eventually move out of the house, you will have more options: more opportunities for prayer and traditional acts of piety, more ways to help others in the Church and the community.

My husband and I are in that state of life now. Our parents have died, and our children have moved on. We now have the peace and leisure for praying and reading good spiritual books and Scripture as much as we want. In fact, a priest friend said he sometimes desires the life of a monk, and he commented that our home would make an excellent monastery! We also have more time to help our children, grandchildren, or neighbors as needed.

As Scripture reminds us, there is a season for everything. Eventually you will have a season that does not involve nursing and caring for your young children. But when we have babies, other children, and a husband, our obligations are primarily to take good care of them. For most of us, in these times, holiness is usually achieved in the ordinary, simple things.

By saying a morning offering prayer each day, you will have already offered up everything you do during the day for the Lord. You will have offered up all your "prayers, works, joys, and sufferings" to the Sacred Heart through the Immaculate Heart of Mary. In other words, everything you do that day can become a prayer. Even the simple act of breastfeeding your baby becomes a prayer.

Before you retire at night, you can say a prayer with your husband. It doesn't have to be a long prayer. It doesn't have to be original. My husband and I say the *Memorare* for our children, sons-in-law, and grandchildren. This is a good time for both spouses to make a recommitment to each other. My husband and I have a habit, when retiring for the night, of finding each other's hand and saying, "I love you" or any other special thought that occurs before going to sleep.

Thus, every task or activity in the home, including breastfeeding your baby or just having a good conversation with your husband, can become a prayer, if you offer it to God as part of the vocation he called you to fulfill with love.

∞

Appendix

∞

The Madonna Rosary

In the fall of 2003, I gave a talk on breastfeeding to a group of priests. Father Timothy Sauppé, an Illinois parish priest, was in the audience and was stirred by the Holy Spirit to write a paper on breastfeeding for a course at the Marian Institute in Dayton, Ohio.

Father Sauppé was aware of the contraceptive influences among his parishioners, and he wanted to counteract those influences by bringing about a culture of life through the motherhood of Mary. He created a Madonna chapel on his church grounds with the Blessed Sacrament present, and he hung pictures of the nursing Madonna on the chapel walls. He provided educational materials in the chapel to inform his parishioners about Catholic moral teaching, Natural Family Planning, sterilization reversals, breast-feeding, and motherhood. Through his Madonna chapel, Father Sauppé preaches to his parishioners about the value of having children and of breastfeeding.

Father Sauppé also came up with the Madonna Rosary to spread devotion to the Blessed Mother's maternity and to encourage us to follow the gospel message.

Use ordinary rosary beads to say this Rosary, but pray the following variation of the Hail Mary and meditate on the Five Mysteries of the Maternity of Mary.

Breastfeeding and Catholic Motherhood

Hail Mary,
full of grace,
the Lord is with thee;
blessed art thou among women, and
blessed is the fruit of thy womb, Jesus.

Holy Mary,
mother of God,
blessed is the womb that carried Jesus
and the breasts that nursed him.
Blessed are those who hear
the Word of God and keep it.

The Five Mysteries of the Maternity of Mary

The Quickening: the Blessed Mother feels Jesus' first movements in the womb.

His First Nursing: the Blessed Mother gives her infant his first nourishment.

His First Steps: Jesus takes his first steps toward his destiny.

His First Words: Jesus speaks for the first time.

Jesus Is Weaned: the last breast-fed bond between Mother and Son.

This Rosary can be prayed individually, or with family members or friends, or in a church setting. If you meet with other Catholic mothers and their little ones for spiritual support, you might consider praying the Madonna Rosary together. If you can't pray all five decades because the children become too much of a distraction during prayer, try to pray at least one decade.

∞

Endnotes

[1] John Paul II, Address to Dr. Nafis Sadik, Secretary General of the 1994 International Conference on Population and Development, March 18, 1994, n. 8.

[2] Cf. Pope John Paul II, Letter to Families, *Gratissimam sane*, February 2, 1994, n. 16.

[3] Breastfeeding rates are low in the United States. Maybe the following will help to explain why. An international program, called the Baby-Friendly Hospital Initiative, began in 1991. This program is "breastfeeding-friendly" because it is based on implementing the "Ten Steps to Successful Breastfeeding" in maternity facilities. Hospitals and birthing centers that promote, protect, and support breastfeeding via the Ten Steps are given "Baby-Friendly" Awards. Over 18,000 hospitals and birthing centers have received this award, yet only forty-two hospitals in the United States had received this award by the end of 2004. In areas where breastfeeding is promoted through the Baby-Friendly Hospital Initiative, the rates of breastfeeding and exclusive breastfeeding go up. Interested persons can learn more about the program at www.babyfriendlyusa.org.

[4] Sheila Kippley, *Breastfeeding and Natural Child Spacing* (Cincinnati: The Couple to Couple League, 1999).

5   Karol Wojtyla, *Love and Responsibility* (New York: Farrar, Straus, and Giroux, 1981), 247.

6   Ibid., 246.

7   Paul VI, *Humanae Vitae* (Of Human Life), trans. Janet E. Smith, *CCL Family Foundations*, July-August 1998.

8   John Paul II, *Evangelium Vitae* (The Gospel of Life), Origins, April 6, 1995.

9   In his book *Dr. Jack Newman's Guide to Breastfeeding*, Newman, a popular speaker at breastfeeding conferences, states, "Breastfeeding should *never* be expendable. Only under extraordinary circumstances should breastfeeding be interrupted. It is too important to the physical and mental health of the child and the mother for them to give it up the way one might give up ice cream. . . . It is worth making the effort to overcome challenges such as sore nipples or a premature baby's weak suckling reflex so that breastfeeding can succeed. And it is equally important to make the changes needed in our medical system and our society so that breastfeeding becomes easier and more acceptable. . . . Each mother who has a happy, successful breastfeeding experience brings us one step closer to a society where breastfeeding is, once again, the norm" (Jack Newman, M.D., and Teresa Pitman, *The Ultimate Breastfeeding Book of Answers* ([title of U.S. edition] Prima Lifestyles, 2000), 6.

10 Promotional business card of La Leche League International: "I'm giving my baby the best start in life!"

11 Linda Smith, "Wondrous Magical Mother's Milk," La Leche League Indiana State Conference, Lebanon, Indiana, November 8, 2003. (Smith's references: Infant Formula Act of 1980;

Robert Jensen, *Handbook of Milk Composition* [San Francisco: Academic Press, 1995].)

[12] American Academy of Family Physicians (AAFP), "Breast-feeding (Position Paper)," 2005. Available at www.aafp.org.

[13] American Academy of Pediatrics (AAP), Policy Statement on Breastfeeding: "Breastfeeding and the Use of Human Milk," *Pediatrics* 100:6 (December 1997) and at www.aap.org.

[14] United States Breastfeeding Committee (USBC), "Benefits of Breastfeeding" (2002) and "Economic Benefits of Breastfeeding" (2002). Available at www.usbreastfeeding.org.

[15] AAFP, "Breastfeeding," 2.

[16] USBC, "Benefits," 3.

[17] USBC, "Economic Benefits," 1.

[18] A. Lucas and T. J. Cole, "Breast milk and neonatal necrotising enterocolitis," Lancet (UK) 336, no. 8730 (Dec 22-29, 1990): 1519-1523.

[19] UNICEF, "Breastfeeding: Foundation for a Healthy Future," August 1999, 1. Available from UNICEF, 3 United Nations Plaza, H-9F, New York, NY 10017, or at www.unicef.org.

[20] A. Bener, S. Denic, and S. Galadari, "Longer Breastfeeding and Protection Against Childhood Leukaemia and Lymphomas," *European Journal of Cancer* 37 (2001): 234-238.

[21] C. Owen, P. Whincup, K. Odoki, J. Gilig, and D. Cook, "Infant Feeding and Blood Cholesterol: A Study in Adolescents and a Systematic Review," *Pediatrics* 110:3 (September 2002): 597-608.

[22] F. Ottoboni and A. Ottoboni, "Can Attention Deficit-Hyperactivity Disorder Result from Nutritional Deficiency?" *Journal of American Physicians and Surgeons* 8:2 (Summer 2003): 58-60.

[23] L. Jacobsson, M. Jacobsson, J. Askling, and W. Knowler, "Perinatal Characteristics and Risk of Rheumatoid Arthritis," *British Medical Journal* 2003, 326: 1068-1069 (May 17, 2003).

[24] A. Lucas, et al., "Breast Milk and Subsequent Intelligence Quotient in Children Born Preterm," *Lancet* 339 (February 1, 1992): 261-264.

[25] L. Horwood and D. Fertusson, "Breastfeeding and Later Cognitive and Academic Outcomes," *Pediatrics* 101:1 (January 1998).

[26] E. Mortensen, K. Michaelsen, S. Sanders, and J. Reinisch, "The Association Between Duration of Breastfeeding and Adult Intelligence," *Journal of the American Medical Association* 287:18 (May 8, 2002): 2365-2371.

[27] Laurence Grummer-Strawn and Zuguo Mei, "Does Breastfeeding Protect Against Pediatric Overweight? Analysis of Longitudinal Data from the Centers for Disease Control and Prevention Pediatric Nutrition Surveillance System," *Pediatrics* 113:2 (February 2004): 81-86.

[28] USBC, "Economic Benefits."

[29] AAP Policy Statement on Breastfeeding.

[30] Ibid.

[31] V. Beral, et al., Collaborative Group on hormonal factors in breast cancer: "Breast cancer and breastfeeding: collaborative

analysis of individual data from 47 epidemiological studies in 30 countries, including 50,302 women with breast cancer and 96,973 women without the disease," *The Lancet* 360:187-195 (July 20, 2002).

³² USBC, "Economic Benefits."

³³ AAFP, "Breastfeeding."

³⁴ *Evangelium Vitae*, sects. 6, 11, 59, 88, 91, 92, and 94.

³⁵ At the fourteenth International La Leche League Conference in 1995, Ken Magid, who works with high-risk children, said this about breastfeeding: "The home is where 'being wanted' starts. The home of the newborn is at the breast of the mother."

³⁶ Sheila Kippley, *The Crucial First Three Years*, available at the website www.NaturalFamilyPlanningAndMore.org.

³⁷ Elliott Barker, *The Greatest Cruelty*, The Canadian Society for the Prevention of Cruelty to Children, Box 700, Midland, Ontario; L4R 4P4 Canada.

³⁸ Ibid.

³⁹ William Gairdner, *The War Against the Family* (Toronto: Stoddart Publishing Co. Limited, 1993).

⁴⁰ Ibid., 340.

⁴¹ Ibid., 338.

⁴² Robin Karr-Morse and Meredith Wiley, *Ghosts from the Nursery: Tracing the Roots for Violence* (New York: The Atlantic Monthly Press, 1997), 7.

⁴³ Ibid., 189.

44 Ken Magid and Carole McKelvey, *High Risk: Children Without a Conscience* (Golden, Colorado: M&M Publishing, 1987), 3.

45 Ken Magid, "Nurturing Children to Become Loving Adults," Fourteenth International La Leche League Convention, 1995.

46 Ibid.

47 Anne Gearan, "High Court Revisits Executing Teen Killers," *The Cincinnati Enquirer*, January 27, 2004.

48 Maria Montessori, *The Absorbent Mind* (New York: Dell Publishing, 1967), 106.

49 Ibid., 104-105.

50 David Blankenhorn, Fellowship of Catholic Scholars Convention, September 24, 1999.

51 Gairdner, 339.

52 Herbert Ratner, *Nature, the Physician, and the Family*, Catholic Physicians Guild of Chicago, December 1997.

53 United States Breastfeeding Committee, "Breastfeeding and Child Care," 2002.

54 "Pope: Women Have 'Special' Role," *The Cincinnati Enquirer*, June 7, 2003.

55 John Paul II, "Women, Wives, and Mothers," *Familia et Vita*, Vatican City, January 1995, 14.

56 Ibid., 13.

57 Ibid., 14.

58 Pius XII, "Guiding Christ's Little Ones," *The Major Addresses of Pope Pius XII*, ed. Vincent A. Yzermans (St. Paul: The North Central Publishing, 1961), 42.

59 Ibid., 43.

60 Ibid.

61 Ibid., 42.

62 Mothers who stay home with their children are heroines, especially in our society, where one's value is measured in terms of career or money earned. With daycare, divorce, illegitimacy, child abuse, and abortion/infanticide, Andrew Thomas said, "Children see a powerful moral to this story . . . that money and sex are life's supreme goals. [Children] are taught, literally from the cradle, that life is looking out for number one" (Andrew Peyton Thomas, *Crime and the Sacking of America* [Washington: Brassey's, 1994], 170).

63 William Virtue, *Mother and Infant: The Moral Theology of Embodied Self-Giving in Motherhood in Light of the Examplar Couplet Mary and Jesus Christ*, dissertation, Pontifical University of St. Thomas, Rome, 1995.

64 Ibid., 278.

65 Ibid., 269.

66 Ibid., 277.

67 Phone conversation, June 8, 1995.

68 Virtue, *Mother and Infant*, 272.

69 Pius XII, *The Major Addresses of Pope Pius XII*, 44.

[70] John Paul II, Address to Dr. Nafis Sadik.

[71] John Paul II, "Breastfeeding: Science and Society," May 11-13, 1995, Pontificiae Academiae Scientiarum Documenta 28, Summary Report of the Pontificia Academia Scientiarum and The Royal Society. In his talk, the Pope endorsed the UNICEF recommendations for infant feeding at that time: exclusive breastfeeding for four to six months and to nurse "up to the second year of life or beyond."

There are two points to be made here. First, today UNICEF strongly recommends exclusive breastfeeding for six months. The Pope, having endorsed the UNICEF recommendations in 1995, would most likely endorse the current UNICEF recommendations of six months of exclusive breastfeeding if he covered this topic again.

Second, the wording by UNICEF of "up to the second year or beyond" was ambiguous. Did this mean that a mother should nurse for one year plus one day so she would be nursing at the beginning of the second year of life, or did it mean a mother should nurse for at least two years? Miriam Labbok, representing UNICEF, clarified the confusion: "WHO and UNICEF support early and exclusive breastfeeding for six months, and continued breastfeeding with age-appropriate complementary feeding for two years or longer" (September 27, 2004 by e-mail).

[72] James McHugh, "Address to the Holy Father," given at the conference "Breastfeeding: Science and Society," May 12, 1995. This fairly recent endorsement of breastfeeding by an American bishop is more welcome. It needs to be said, however, that exclusive breastfeeding is not sufficient by itself to guarantee breastfeeding infertility during the first six months postpartum, as Bishop Hugh suggested in his talk. I have spent more than

thirty years telling parents and professionals that exclusive breastfeeding during the first six months of life is only one rule among the seven rules or standards that need to be followed for achieving normal breastfeeding infertility. The Seven Standards are discussed in chapter 6.

[73] Alfonso Cardinal López Trujillo, "Foreword," *Breastfeeding and Natural Child Spacing* (The Couple to Couple League, 1999).

[74] Al Lauer, "The Courage to Be Myself," *One Bread, One Body,* February 5, 2004.

[75] Timothy Sauppé, "Art and the Parish Madonna Chapel," unpublished paper, International Marian Research Institute, University of Dayton, February 6, 2004, 2.

[76] Even philosophers can promote breastfeeding. In the fall of 2003, a Catholic philosopher told my husband and me that he uses breastfeeding to teach God's design in his classes. His students enjoyed this approach.

[77] Some scientists over the years have seen the relationship between the placenta and the breasts of the mother. This explanation is nothing new. For example, in November 1985, Dr. Peter Howie at the Fourth National and International Symposium on Natural Family Planning called the breast "the postnatal placenta."

[78] World Health Organization, "Infant and young child nutrition," Fifty-Fifth World Health Assembly, April 16, 2002.

[79] Karr-Morse and Wiley, *Ghosts from the Nursery,* 207.

[80] Nils Bergman, "Kangaroo Mother Care," Tri-State Breastfeeding Advocates Seminar, August 29, 2003, Cincinnati, Ohio.

[81] A 1994 note sent to us on our anniversary by one of our children shows the spiritual and emotional value for children, no matter what their age, when Mom and Dad remain together: "Mom and Dad, I just wanted you both to know how happy I am that you two have loved each other and devoted your lives to each other and to our family. It means the world to me that my parents are married and that my only conception of what a family is, is one family with two parents living in one house. I feel very blessed to have parents who care about family and marriage. It means a lot to me. I wish so many of my other friends could have been able to grow up in one household where the parents love each other and are kind and considerate to one another. The Kippley kids are very fortunate to have the understanding that marriage is a covenant for life, and it is mostly because of your own example."

[82] Virtue, *Mother and Infant*, 228-229.

[83] Wojtyla, *Love and Responsibility*, 38.

[84] Ibid., 131.

[85] Ibid., 226.

[86] Sheila Kippley, *Integrating Faith and Science Through NFP*, "Comparison of Ecological Breastfeeding with Lactation Amenorrhea Method," ed. Richard Fehring and Theresa Notare (Milwaukee: Marquette University Press, 2004), 218-219.

[87] Breastfeeding provides comfort to your baby and is an easy way to satisfy your baby's sucking needs to put him to sleep. Research shows that the use of pacifiers usually shortens the

nursing time at the breast, shortens the duration of breastfeeding, and shortens the duration of infertility.

[88] Most mothers need lots of strong periodic stimulation from the baby's nursing to keep the reproductive cycle at rest. A few working mothers may go a year without a period while pumping their milk and by nursing their baby before and after work and all through the night, but that is an exception. Some parents can't picture caring for a baby without bottles and pacifiers. We cared for four babies without the use of pacifiers or bottles and did not miss them.

There is nothing wrong with using bottles or pacifiers, but they are not compatible with the Seven Standards and should be avoided by those parents who want to enjoy extended breastfeeding infertility. A pacifier or bottle used for that rare occasion is okay, but often the "rare" use becomes a regular practice and the mother may soon feel that she does not have enough milk. If this happens, the mother can eliminate the bottles or pacifiers, or both, and increase the nursing to reverse the situation so that she once again has an ample milk supply for her baby. The greater the demand by the baby at the breast, the better the milk supply will be.

[89] Nursing is one job many mothers learn to do in their sleep. Sharing sleep with your baby, while not an essential part of breastfeeding, is very helpful in maintaining amenorrhea, and it is a safe practice when done properly. Information on sleeping with your baby, including safety guidelines, can be found at www.cosleeping.org.

Sleeping with a nursing baby can have a tremendous impact upon the length of amenorrhea for some mothers. For example, one mother nursed her babies without pacifiers or bottles, and her babies slept in the crib during the night. With her first three babies, menstruation returned by seven months post-partum. When she read *Breastfeeding and Natural Child Spacing,* she and her husband bought a king-size bed, and they decided to sleep with their fourth baby. Her menstruation returned at twenty months with her fourth baby; she attributes this difference to her co-sharing sleep with her baby. Similar differences in the return of fertility have been reported by other mothers. What changes is their mothering practices.

[90] You can use the rest, and this is one time your baby can nurse at his leisure without interruption. You will also have a more ample milk supply if you are not fatigued but well rested. For information on the benefits of the Seven Standards, see *Breastfeeding and Natural Child Spacing.*

[91] Consensus statement: "Breastfeeding as a Family Planning Method," *The Lancet* (November 19, 1988), 1204-1205.

[92] In over thirty years of looking at breastfeeding charts, my husband and I have yet to see a fertile ovulation or a pregnancy charted during the first three months while a nursing mother follows the Seven Standards.

[93] "Breastfeeding as a Family Planning Method," 1204-1205.

[94] Sheila and John Kippley, "The Spacing of Babies with Ecological Breastfeeding," *International Review* (Spring/Summer 1989): 107-116.

[95] Sheila and John Kippley, *The Art of Natural Family Planning* (Cincinnati: The Couple to Couple League, 1996).

[96] New Hope Publications, 2003.

⁹⁷ La Leche League, *The Womanly Art of Breastfeeding,* seventh edition (Schaumburg, Illinois, 2004).

⁹⁸ J. Ballard, C. Auer, and J. Khoury, "Ankyloglossia: Assessment, Incidence, and Effect of Frenuloplasty on the Breastfeeding Dyad," *Pediatrics* 110:5 (November 2002).

⁹⁹ T. Ball and A. Wright, "Health Care Costs of Formula-feeding in the First Year of Life," *Pediatrics* 103:4 (April 1999).

¹⁰⁰ J. Raisler, C. Alexander, and P. O'Campo, "Breast-Feeding and Infant Illness: A Dose-Response Relationship," *American Journal of Public Health* 89:1 (January 1999).

¹⁰¹ American Academy of Family Physicians: www.aafp.org.

¹⁰² Newman, *Dr. Jack Newman's Guide to Breastfeeding,* 205.

¹⁰³ I might have earned more money than my husband. However, we made the decision that I should be home with the children. When John wanted to pursue further studies, I was pregnant with our fourth child. John assumed I would work while he went to school. I said no. I did not want to leave the children. He agreed with my position, and fortunately, an excellent job opportunity developed for him, and plans changed.

I have saved one letter to an editor. It was written to show the importance of being a stay-at-home mother. It was quite lengthy, but the ending is what I remember and will share with you. This mother wrote, "I knew what it was like to be a latch-key child before the term was invented. I was brave for a mother who went to work instead of being there for her kids. I put on a brave front because I loved her and wanted to make her happy. I was scared most of the time, lonely and without a champion when I needed one. I would live in a dirt shack before I would not be there for my kids" (Cindy Standley, "Stay-at-Home Moms Champion Their Worth," *The Cincinnati Enquirer*, November 11, 1997).

[104] My husband and I developed the website www.NaturalFamily PlanningAndMore.org primarily to promote Natural Family Planning, as well as Catholic teaching and devotions. You may contact us at this website.

Sheila Kippley

For over forty years Sheila Kippley has been an advocate for breast-feeding, mother-child togetherness, and Natural Family Planning. Her two books, *Breastfeeding and Natural Child Spacing* and *The Art of Natural Family Planning* (co-authored with her husband, John), are classics in their field.

The Kippleys have raised five children and have ten grand-children. They can be contacted at their website: www.Natural FamilyPlanningAndMore.org.